Arthur Bott

Prussia and the German System of Education

Arthur Bott

Prussia and the German System of Education

ISBN/EAN: 9783337170752

Printed in Europe, USA, Canada, Australia, Japan

Cover: Foto ©Suzi / pixelio.de

More available books at **www.hansebooks.com**

PRUSSIA

AND THE

GERMAN SYSTEM OF EDUCATION.

BY

ARTHUR BOTT.

Read before the Albany Institute, February, 1867.

ALBANY, N. Y.:

JOEL MUNSELL.

1868.

PRUSSIA

AND THE

GERMAN SYSTEM OF EDUCATION.

The power which now speaks to Europe in the name of Germany, and which certainly bids fair to unite all German states under her sceptre, was unknown at the period of the Reformation.

The counts of Hohenzollern descend from tributaries of Charlemagne. Their house long maintained a precarious existence as a fief of Poland. From the beginning, it clutched at every territory within its reach, swallowed up the smaller ones wherever found, near or far, and left to time the consolidation of the fragments into one organic body. If proprietors of intervening territory could not be subdued, they were cheated in barter or caught in the meshes of Venus. From the swamps of Brandenburg, hardly larger than an English county, the counts of Hohenzollern dotted western and northern Germany with these demesnes. The Jülich and Cleve duchies lay leagues away from Brandenburg, as Brandenburg was far away from Stettin; and none of them had any topographical connection with eastern Prussia. All these acquisitions were rather the outposts of a projected kingdom than vital members of one political body. In every European treaty Prussia secured some new dominion. Early in the eighteenth century Austria permitted her to

1

assume a royal dignity. This was the crisis of her history. The sword of Frederic, by incorporating Silesia and Posen, raised her from a feudatory of Austria, to a powerful rival; and while the latter still hugged the rude old feudal system, Prussia, by employing every new, wise principle of national progress, obtained the commercial, and through this, the political control of all Germany. In her enlightened system of public education, her commercial codes based on strict reciprocity; by political representation and the widest religious freedom; she presents, beside the neighboring despotism, all the contrast of science with ignorance, of integrity with corruption, of light with darkness.

In her political alliances, Prussia has one principle — that of a selfish expediency. She accepts the hand of either belligerent, like a partner in a dance. She has kidnapped the states which she could not honorably annex, as Frederic kidnapped recruits for his giant regiment. She has trampled on every principle of international law and perpetrated every crime necessary to her ends. She instigated and mainly procured the dismemberment of Poland. Her own original fief was torn from the knights whose interests she had sworn, as chief and guardian, to defend. Two of the most important members of the empire were seized by acts of buccaneering unsurpassed in the history of nations. While accepting British money to despatch troops to Austerlitz, she was negotiating with Napoleon for British Hanover as the price of neutrality. She pledged herself to Napoleon to guard the rear of his Russian army and then fulfilled the pledge by turning thirty thousand bayonets against his frozen, perishing fugitives. Treacherous to the last, she made a tool of Austria to subdue Schleswig-Holstein and then seized the whole prize, kicked Austria out of doors, and ground the whole confederation to dust.

But she has characteristics which might redeem her rapacity. Her kings and electors have been frugal, even to parsimony, in their households — not for family aggrandizement but to lighten the public burdens and to create an efficient civil and military department. They have melted their plate, slept on hard beds, dressed in frieze, eaten peasant's food, to keep the national expenses within the receipts. William I. sold his jewels, sent his spoons to the mint, abolished the costly court ceremonies, even dismissed the wig-maker and barber, in order to establish a school for the army. As a consequence, Prussia shows, up to this day, the cleanest yearly balance sheet of Europe. While other nations become insolvent in peace, Prussia clears off her debts even in time of war. New states are made to pay the expenses of their own annexation. The sinking fund will remove the present indebtedness within twelve years. This personal interest thus extended to the people by their rulers gives a peculiar freedom to the life of the latter; absolute in its social and religious elements and yet modified by the sovereign's paternal care. A Jew may guide the Prussian parliament, a Roman Catholic may mount the throne. To every child in the land, of either sex, however remote or however poor, the government furnishes freely seven years of sound, generous education. The Prussian people thus enjoy all the splendid advantages of a great empire with the financial ease and social and religious liberty of a petty state. Although the countries which she has violently seized, struggled at first like the Sabine women, they now seem only to desire the closest intimacy with their captors. Certainly they have gained much and lost little by their change of masters.

ADMINISTRATION OF PUBLIC INSTRUCTION.

The administration of Schools was centralized only in the present century, by transferring it to the Ministry of the Interior. Here it was placed under the immediate direction of William Humboldt, as State Councillor. Since 1817, Educational and Ecclesiastical matters have formed a special Ministerial department.

Under this Central Department, stand eight Provincial Administrations, which recognize local and sectarian peculiarities. In each Province, a Deputation regulates all the internal affairs of church and school ; determining the general object of the educational institutions ; examining their statutes and discipline ; proposing plans of improvement and designating text-books; supervising the higher schools and appointing or removing teachers. The provincial boards manage the property of church and school and regulate the elementary and primary departments of the latter, and report to the Minister six commissions, distinct from these Boards, examine teachers for the higher schools, and revise the examinations for graduation. Each commission has seven members ; one for each of the following branches — Philology, History, Mathematics and Physics, Science of Teaching, Theology, and Hebrew, Natural Sciences, Modern Languages.

By the Prussian constitution, all schools and universities are declared Institutions of the State ; they cannot be established without the consent of the state and are subject to its supervision ; they are open to all sects but persons dissenting from their religious system are not required to attend the religious instruction ; schools and Gymnasia for the higher sciences and the arts and trades, enjoy the same powers as corporations and are controlled immediately by the state authorities ; teachers not appointed by persons or corporations, through legacy or special privilege, are appointed by the state; schools conducted by private persons or corporations are subject to supervision of the Provincial Boards, as to their teachers and discipline and instruction. Also, the supervisors must dissuade persons evidently incompetent, from entering the learned professions; they must encourage and aid youth of superior talent; no dismissal can take place, without a testimonial of mental and moral character. The mode of education of the child is left to the father's choice, but the necessary instruction in religion and useful knowledge according to his position must be imparted. Any person may instruct, after authorization by the state. Teachers of the Gymnasia and other higher schools are declared officers of the state.

In Germany, education is compulsory on both sexes, for seven years from the child's sixth or seventh year. This education is merely elementary. The state, however, is obliged to prepare the individual for his future vocation.

In the large cities, free schools especially for the poorer classes are maintained by the municipality aided by the state; all teachers are appointed by the government and the municipality jointly, and the schools are supported by the latter.

In 1857, Prussia contained 27,963 elementary schools with over 30,000 teachers and 2,859,694 scholars; and 1,171 private schools, with 3,635 teachers and 83,021 scholars; leaving about 11,000 non-attendants. In France, at the same time, nearly one-third of the children of proper age were non-attendants and another third attended school during a few months of the year only.

Prussia has long paid special attention to its Normal system. It honors teaching as a regular profession. The teacher consequently loves his calling with enthusiasm. In the higher schools of the cities, he associates with the *elite.* In the elementary and the village schools, he and the pastor are the gentlemen of the place. He considers himself not as laboring for a livelihood but as shaping the destinies of his nation. He retains his position, generally during life, growing old among his own pupils, whose reverent affection breathes over his declining years an idyllic charm.

The Normal Seminaries contain 39 protestant and 16 catholic instructors with 2,600 students. Before entering, the student must pass examination in the three lower branches of the Gymnasium, at least. The course lasts three years and embraces all the branches of the common school course, but especially the science of education and catechetics. The instruction is practical; the pupils applying daily their principles, under the supervision of the professors, in instructing the pupils of the schools connected with the seminary. At graduation, they pass a rigid examination *pro facultate docendi*, and enter the service of the state according to their several qualifications.

The examination *pro facultate docendi* comprises German Latin, Greek, French and Hebrew; mathematics, physics, natural history; history and geography, antiquities, mythology, history of Greek and Roman literature; philosophy and theology. It is conducted before the royal commission, is both oral and written, and includes a trial-lesson in one of the higher classes of the Gymnasium. Lately, a trial year has been introduced, to secure fuller proficiency.

There are a few seminaries for the preparation of teachers for the higher schools. Their course follows that of the University and presumes a previous complete scientific education, and a degree *pro facultate docendi*. They are connected more or less closely with the University and seek less to teach the art of teaching than to produce independent application and development of science. A Philological seminary is connected with every university. Philosophical, historical or mathematical seminaries are

rare. Students stay two years, rarely four. They com-
pose educational and scientific treatises, and criticise them
in special conferences. They take classes in the Gymnasia
or study the methods of certain teachers and practice under them.

The Grammar schools are exclusively designed to prepare the sons of citizens for the pursuits of common life.
Admission takes place at the ninth year, and presumes
facility in reading German and Roman print, knowledge
of the parts of speech, a readable and clear hand-writing,
fair spelling, knowledge of the four fundamental rules of
Arithmetic and acquaintance with the narratives of the
old and the new Testament. After six years, the pupil is
expected to write good German, to translate correctly
from other tongues, to understand thoroughly the Latin
grammar, and read well Cesar and Ovid ; to pronounce
correctly English and French and write them freely from
dictation ; to know the outlines of general history, the
most important events of Greek and Roman history, and
especially that of Germany and Prussia since the Thirty
years war. He must be acquainted with the most important conditions of the earth's surface, with the topical and
political geography of Europe and especially with that of
Germany and Prussia; with the elements of Mathematical
Geography, the chief botanical, zoölogical and mineralo-
gical systems, the physiology and anatomy of the plants
and animals especially valuable in commerce and the arts,
the general properties of bodies, the laws of heat, the
elements of Chemistry, Geometry, Stereometry, Plane
Trigonometry, Equations, Logarithms, and Progressions.

There are countries in Germany in which the school
system is even more rigidly enforced than in Prussia.
Wurtemberg, for instance, with its University, its primary
schools established in every hamlet, its compulsory education of children from the 6th to 14th year, has given

birth to a greater number of scholars and literary men than any other land; among them. Schiller Wieland, Uhland, Schubart, Kerner, Knapp, Schelling and Hegel.

The Schools of Industry and Arts (Real Schulen), are public institutions in which especial attention is paid to instruction in natural sciences and mathematics, and which prepare their pupils for practical life. They treat ancient languages as secondary and give to the natural sciences, geography, chemistry, history, technology, mathematics and modern languages the first rank. They dismiss their pupils to the military, postal, forest and architectural schools and services, and to all professions for which a University education is not required. There are 83 real schools with 1,037 teachers.

The following is the plan of study and number of hours per day allotted to each branch.

		CLASSES.					
		VI.	V.	IV.	III.	II.	I.
Religion,............Hours per Week,		3	3	2	2	2	2
German,..................... "		4	4	3	3	3	3
Latin,....................... "		8	6	6	5	4	3
French,..................... "			5	5	4	4	4
English,.................... "					4	3	3
Geography and history,... "		3	3	4	4	3	3
Natural sciences,........... "		2	2	2	2	6	6
Geometry and arithmetic, "		5	4	6	6	5	5
Penmanship,... .... "		3	2	2			
Drawing,..................... "		2	2	2	2	2	3
		30	31	32	32	32	32

Before leaving the school, the pupil must pass a thorough examination, both oral and written; the latter consisting of a German, French and English composition, a translation into the Latin, the solving of two arithmetical and two geometrical problems and a treatise on some theme in Natural Philosophy and on another in Chemistry; the oral examination testing his acquirements in religion, history, geography, mathematics and the natural sciences. In the German language, the student must be able to work out a theme in logical order and in correct, good language. He must also speak the language correctly and fluently, and must be acquainted with the principal periods of German literature. In Latin, he must be able to translate into good German, portions of Cæsar, Sallust, Livy, Ovid and Virgil, read before. In French and English he must possess a thorough knowledge of grammar and be able to write an exercise and a dictation from the German without strong Germanism or grammatical mistakes. He must also converse with some facility in these languages and have some acquaintance with their literature. He must have a systematic knowledge of universal history and general chronology. In natural philosophy he must know its laws and fundamental ideas, as well as the methods of experiment ; the laws of gravitation and motion ; the principles of heat, electricity, magnetism, sound and light. In chemistry and oryctognosy is required a knowledge, based upon experiments, of the affinities of the more common inorganic and organic substances. The student must be able to describe and to employ the best processes for the more common chemical products and also to state the nature and uses of the latter. He must exercise a scientific knowledge of the whole field of mathematics, as algebra, proportions, equations, progression, binomial theorems, logarithms, plane trigonometry, stereometry, descriptive and analytic geometry, conic sections, statics, and mechanics.

The Polytechnic Schools prepare their pupils by scientific instruction for the arts and technical professions. They differ from the common schools of art or industry in that they enter more systematically into the technical sciences, and presuppose a complete course of the mathematical and natural sciences. They differ from other schools of learning in their manifold relations to industrial life; they treat their subjects no less scientifically but at the same time furnish opportunities for practical applications. The instruction comprises a three-years course after the manner of academies or universities; the pupil selecting his own branches. This course is divided into two parts; the first being the technical, teaching the lower and higher branches of mathematics, physics and mechanism, general chemistry, machinery and drawing. This section is subdivided into three faculties for engineering, machine-building and technical chemistry. The students in the first, study also, the higher sciences of surveying, hydraulics, road and railroad architecture, and construct plans; those of the second are instructed in mechanism, machine-building and mechanical technology, and the planning of single machines and whole factories; and those of the third, study physics, theoretical and analytical chemistry and chemical technology and practice chemical analyses and preparations. Some branches of jurisprudence and political economy, as well as modern languages, being of equal importance to all the faculties, are taught in them all. The second section is the commercial and comprise the instruction in mercantile correspondence, in commercial sciences, commercial laws and laws of exchange, in mercantile calculations and book-keeping, in commercial geography and history and modern languages. At the end of each term, an examination is held and testimonials are given according to its result.

Germany possesses 24 schools for architecture, 12 for mining, 17 for forestry (arboriculture etc.), 31 for commerce, 46 military schools, 70 for agriculture, 10 for music, 81 naval schools, 12 veterinary schools, 12 surgical, 64 for various other sciences.

THE UNIVERSITIES OF GERMANY.

Universities were first founded in Germany in the 13th century. They were modeled after the high schools of the Arabs in Bagdad, Cordova, Salamanca, Seville, Toledo, and Alexandria. The studies were grammar, poetry, philosophy, law, medicine, astronomy, mathematics and practical sciences.

The Universities are the pride and glory of Germany. They exert more influence there than similar institutions in any other country. They are the centres of the higher intellectual and literary life of the nation and the laboratories of new theories of action. They reflect a picture; the whole world of nature and of mind under its ideal form. They develop the talents and form the principles of nearly all who fill the places of power in church and state, from the village pastor to the oberconsistorialrath, from the advocate at the bar to the head of the cabinet. They receive the best minds from the lowest as well as the highest ranks and fit them for public usefulness.

From them, emanate principally the ideas and maxims whether conservative or progressive which rule the land.

It is characteristic that the Reformation in Germany, proceeded, not from princes and bishops as in England, but from theological professors.

The great philosophical and theological revolution of the last century and the counter revolution of the present century, have likewise proceeded mainly from the studies and lecture rooms of the academic teachers.

Such supremacy of literary institutions and literary men has, however, its disadvantages. It could not exist in a country like ours or England, where politics and commerce engage so large a proportion of the best talent and energy of the nation. But in Germany, it is closely connected with the genius, history and condition of the people, and no one can form a correct idea of the nation's higher and deeper life without a knowledge of its universities.

Each nation has its peculiar mission and excellency. Ancient Israel was elected to prepare the true religion for the world ; Greece to develop the principles of science and art ; Rome to actualize the idea of law and civil government. So in our times, the chief significance of Germany lies neither in politics nor in war nor in commerce, but in science and literature. The German universities exert also a powerful influence upon other countries.

Situated in the heart of Europe and visited by strangers from all quarters of the globe, they are the strongholds of general learning and literature and of the highest culture of Europe and America.

Twenty six Universities exist in the entire German confederation. Of these, six belong to the kingdom of Prussia (at Berlin, Halle, Bonn, Breslaw, Königsberg, Greisswalde, to which may be added the Roman Catholic High School of Munster) ; six to the Empire of Austria (Vienna, Prague, Olmutz, Gratz, Salzburg, Innsbruck) ; three to the kingdom of Bavaria (Munich, Erlangen, Wurzburg) ; two to the grand Duchy of Baden (Heidelberg and Freiburg) ; one to the kingdom of Wurtemberg (Tübingen) ; one to the kingdom of Saxony (Leipsic).

Eight are Roman Catholic, thirteen Protestant, five of both creeds.

These institutions are maintained by princely or by private donations, by tithes and by annual appropriations of the government. The popes frequently transferred to them the proceeds of a part of the church property. At the Reformation, the wealth of the secularized abbeys and since 1773, that of the order of Jesuits have been largely devoted to them. They are also generally exempt from taxation and enjoy certain temporal privileges. Tuition forms the least source of income. The students pay besides the matriculation fee, a certain sum ($2 to $10) for each course of lectures ; but the chief resource of the professors is a fixed salary paid by the state, ranging from a few hundred to several thousand dollars, according to age, merit and reputation.

The university is divided into four faculties. Each faculty elects annually from itself, its own dean. At the head of the whole academic body, stands the rector or chancellor, likewise chosen annually from the regular professors of each faculty in its turn. The legislative power resides in the academic senate, composed of all the ordinary professors or a delegated number. A university is thus a complete republic of letters, highly independent of church and state, although furnishing to both, all their higher officers. This academic liberty, both intellectual and moral, the utmost liberty to teach and to learn, is cherished as one of the most precious privileges.

The four faculties embrace all the sacred and the secular sciences and make up the idea of a university ; a term which was first applied to the body of teachers and pupils (universitas scholarium), but is now understood mainly of the totality of letters (universitas literarum), and the completeness of the system of instruction.

We now proceed to a separate notice of the four professional schools which form a German University :

1st. The theological faculty still has the supremacy, since, when most of the universities were founded theology was emphatically the queen of sciences. The great institution at Paris was at first simply a theological and philosophical school ; the philosophical studies served as a preparation to scholastic divinity, and the philosophical professors were all ecclesiatics.

In the middle ages, theology was confined to the interpretation of the Latin Bible on the basis of the Catenæ-Patrum and to scholastic dogmatics and ethics, under the guidance of the Sentences of Peter the Lombard, called the "Magister Sententiarum." In modern times, the field has been greatly enlarged by the addition of Oriental philology, biblical criticism, hermeneutics, antiquities, church history and doctrinal history, homiletics, catechetics, liturgics, pastoral theology and theory of church government. No theological faculty is now considered complete without separate professors for the exegetical, historical, systematic and practical branches of divinity. Professors may lecture however, in any department, if not neglecting their immediate duties, Schleiermacher, for instance, taught in turn almost every branch of theology and philosophy.

2d. The Philosophical faculty is by far the most numerous in its teachers and departments; and besides philosophy proper, it embraces history, ancient and modern languages, mathematics, belles lettres. It was formerly called the faculty of Arts (facultas artium liberalium,) whence the terms, Bachelor and Master of Arts.

In the middle ages, all human sciences, as distinct from theology, were divided into seven artes liberales, viz., grammar, rhetoric, dialectics, arithmetic, music, geometry and astronomy.

The first three constituted the Trivium ; the remaining four the Quadrivium. The principal text-books in these departments were the dialectical, ethical and physical works of Aristotle, until the Reformation and the philosophy of Bacon and Cartesius deposed the great Stagyrite from his long reign. Since that time, although the historical, philological and natural sciences have made immense progress, the faculties have not kept pace with them, in their reorganization.

The Philosophical study, properly so called, includes logic, metaphysics, philosophy of nature, anthropology and psychology, philosophy of law or political ethics, philosophy of history, philosophy of art or æsthetics, moral philosophy, philosophy of religion, and history of philosophy.

3d. The faculty of Law (facultas juris canoniciet civilis) embraces a greater variety of studies (especially the history of civil, criminal, and common law, the exposition of the ancient Roman Code, and the canon law) than our own law schools. But on the other hand, these latter, with the many opportunities for public speaking and our republican institutions, produce stronger advocates and more practical statesmen. The German law-schools were modeled after the oldest in the world, that of Bologna.

4. The faculty of Medicine comprehends chemistry, physiology, anatomy, phrenology, pathology and similar sciences, which are taught also in all our regular medical colleges.

The universities of Berlin and Vienna, enjoy the greatest medical reputation.

The system of academical degrees originated likewise in the middle ages. In Germany, the lower degrees have disappeared except for divinity, but the doctorship remains for each faculty. This may be acquired after the completion of the prescribed course, by a special examination, printed dissertation or book and public disputation conducted in Latin; all involving considerable expense. The diploma of Doctor of Philosophy, however, which corresponds somewhat to our Master of Arts, and also that of Doctor of Medicine, can be more easily secured; at least, from several smaller universities. Some years ago, complaint was entered at the Diet of Frankfort against the traffic in the lower diplomas which brought them into disrepute; and the lesser states were compelled to check it. The Prussian universities demand very scrupulously a rigorous examination and public disputation, and never waste a degree honoris causa.

In theology, there are still two degrees, that of the Licentiate (corresponding to the English Bachelor of Divinity), which confers the right of public teaching in the university, and that of D. D. The latter is the highest academic honor and hence much rarer than the doctor's diploma of any other faculty. It may be acquired by the regular process of a written work and Latin debate, in which every member of the university can attack the published theses of the candidate; but it is now generally given honoris causa, as an acknowledgment of distinguished literary merit, or of eminent usefulness in the church.

The Gymnasia, unlike the colleges of England and America, confer no degrees.

There are three classes of teachers in the universities.

1st. The ordinary professors; who are regular members of the faculty and receive a full support from the state independently of the proceeds of their lectures and can be elected to the academical senate and the rectorship.

2d. The extraordinary professors; who have no seat in the faculty nor in the senate, and have a smaller income but are generally promoted to a vacant regular professorship.

3d. The private lecturers (privatim docentes); who have passed through the examen rigorosum and deliver lectures like the regular professors but are without appointment and generally receive no salary from the state. They depend therefore, upon the fees for lectures or private tuition or extra literary labor. Unless they have means of their own or eminent popular talents which attract crowds and secure sometimes a special appropriation from the minister, they drag out a very weary existence.

Most of the professors must pass through these stages before reaching the honor and benefits of a regular or ordinary professorship. Some few distinguished men, however, are called directly, from the ranks of the ministry or of the law or medicine.

The number of teachers varies from thirty to a hundred and fifty or even more. At Berlin, there are 186 professors for 2435 students; at Vienna, 181 professors for 4608 students; at Munich, 119 for 1213 students; at Gottingen 144 for 711 students; at Leipsic 112 for 1007 students; at Heidelberg, 98 for 850 students; at Bonn, 98 for 935 · students; at Breslaw, 101 for 946 students.

One of the most important characteristics of the German university is the professorial or lecture system as distinct from the English tutorial system. Instead of a number of colleges, as in Oxford and Cambridge, where the students live together under moral supervision, one large building with a number of halls (Hörsaal) receives them during a part of the day for the lectures, as they may choose to attend. Attendance is left to their own sense of duty. The studious and conscientious frequent four or five lectures daily. When the clock strikes, they take their seats in the Hörsaal, unfold their portfolios and strike the ink-horn (armed below with a sharp iron spike) into the wooden desk, waiting for the learned oracle. After an intermission of ten or fifteen minutes, the professor ascends the rostrum and with the familiar address, "Meine Herren," begins his lecture standing or sitting, reading or extemporizing or both alternately. Some of the hearers take down in short-hand every word that drops from the mouth of living wisdom. Others show their contempt for goose-quill learning by merely listening or noting the general heads.

The most judicious appropriate the lecture to their mind as it goes on, and reproduce it in a condensed form. If the professor speaks indistinctly, some give him a hint with a motion of their feet, to repeat the sentence. But not all professors pay attention to this linguam pedestrem.

3

Each lecture lasts about three quarters of an hour till the clock gives its accustomed sound, when the professor folds his manuscript, the students wipe their pens, shut the ink horn, take hat or cap and portfolio and crowd to the door, to return to their lodgings or to attend another lecture or to walk the hospitals or enter the laboratories.

This is generally all the instruction imparted in these institutions. In Berlin and Halle, however, meetings (Seminare) are held in the professors' houses for the discussion of Biblical, and patriotic or of classical authors and for the composition of Latin prize essays.

Thus Neander used to read in this familiar way Tertullian's Apolegeticus, Origen's Commentaries and De Principiis, Augustine's Confessions, Chrysostom De Sacerdotio, etc. These meetings are conducted in Latin. In Tubingen, the lecture-system is accompanied by weekly recitations and examinations conducted by the repententen, who may be compared to the tutors or teaching-fellows of British universities.

Until the middle of the eighteenth century, the lectures were all delivered in Latin : a method which was very injurious to the cultivation of the German language. The scholars of the seventeenth century wrote and spoke the classical or the scholastic Latin better than their mother tongue. It was the merit of Thoniasius, professor in Halle, that he began the gradual abolition of this pedantry, and introduced the national language ; at present very few lectures are delivered in Latin, while this language is still used very properly in academic dissertations, the conferring of degrees and other public solemnities.

It is easy to see that the lecture system has great advantages both for the professor and the student. The task of writing one or more learned lectures every day, at least early in the professorial career, draws out all the powers and produces that high scholarship and marvellous literary fertility in which Protestant Germany surpasses all other countries, and by which it furnishes to England and America, directly or indirectly, most of their classical and scientific text books. To the student, this system is generally the most impressive. When a science comes clothed in flesh and blood from the mind and lips of the professor like Minerva from the head of Jove, it inspires the hearer with a consciousness of the creative power slumbering within himself and fires it into action. And the habit of writing, pursued by the student, accompanied by thought is generally the best method of mental appropriation and digestion. But on the other hand, it must be admitted that the German universities promote an excessive individuality of intellect and fertility of opinions ; an extreme opposite to the stagnate steadiness, uniformity and traditionalism of Oxford and Cambridge. If the government allow too little political liberty, the universities allow too great intellectual and doctrinal liberty. With a vast amount of invaluable learning and useful systems they have brought forth also many fantastic, absurd and revolutionary theories.

They have been the hot houses of rationalism, skepticism and pantheism, and all sorts of dangerous innovations.

A model university, while affording the widest cultivation of all sciences, should never lose the great aim of benefiting society and of training the rising intellect for practical usefulness in church and state. It should reconcile the claims of authority and of freedom and guard the unity and harmony of truth as well as the diversity and universality of science. The lecture system can and should be combined with the recitation system — thus ascertaining the student's progress, explaining the subject fully and supplying the peculiar needs of each young mind for its future career in life.

The German universities maintain the principle of universal admission both for those who wish to teach and for those who wish to learn, on the sole condition of intellectual capacity. There are no sectarian or religious disabilities, as at Oxford and Cambridge, except for the professorship of the theological faculty. Thus you find among the students Lutherans, Reformed, Roman Catholics, Greeks and even Jews, and many foreigners from all countries of Europe and America. Here they enter an unlimited field of independent study, where they may for four or more years conduct their education and acquire, on examination, an academic degree.

The students have generally passed their eighteenth or twentieth year when they leave the dull routine of the gymnasium. Their sojourn in the university is an era of perfect intellectual freedom, such as they never enjoy in subsequent life. They choose their profession, their professors and the lectures; they may attend them with scrupulous regularity or waste their precious time in idleness and dissipation. They are supposed to possess full intellectual and moral maturity except in politics. The only compulsion to study are the examinations requisite for the Doctor's diploma or for the active service of church and state. But the strongest stimulus is supposed to be an enthusiasm for science and the highest culture.

The universities are not training schools, like the gymnasia and our American colleges, but they represent the unity and universality of scientific knowledge, the field for the presentation and dissemination of truth; and they afford unlimited opportunity for original study and self development. To many a youth, this academical freedom proves disastrous; but the German student is proverbial for his plodding disposition and his unwearying toil. It must be confessed that drinking, duelling (although the

latter is strictly prohibited) and other lawless and vulgar
habits still disgrace several of these learned institutions,
especially in smaller towns, as Jena and Geissen, where
the students hold the citizens or "Philistines," under
their control. But with proper allowance for national
genius and taste, German students lose nothing by comparison with those of Oxford and Cambridge, while in
industry they generally surpass them.

"A German student," says a recent English writer,
" does not feather his oar in a university boat or regatta
day; he does not kick the foot-ball on Parker's piece ; he
does not skilfully take the balls at a cricket match.

" These gentle pastimes would not satisfy his bolder and
noisier disposition. His thoughts are more excitable and
somewhat enthusiastic. His manners are more cordial
and unreserved. His appearance and demeanor are less
aristocratic. Yet he is well-bred, spirited and high-
minded ; he is frank and open ; a faithful friend and an
eccentric lover of his Fatherland. He is a sworn enemy
to all falsehood and all deceit. Peculiar notions of honor
and a deep love of independence and liberty belong to his
most deep-rooted principles. Song and music, social
parties, convivial fetes, a martial, undaunted spirit, and
excitement of the patriotic feelings throw over his life an
enchantment which gilds it yet in all his later recollections."

The students live not in one building, as is generally
the case in our colleges, but are scattered through the
town. They spend from two to five hours every day in
the lecture rooms and the rest of the time in reading
and writing at home or in intercourse with their fellow
students. The majority, especially the "foxes," as the
fresh-men are called, join the social clubs, the members of
which generally wear or used to wear peculiar colors on
their caps, flags, and breast-bands, and meet on special
days at a particular inn or private room. At their meet-

ings, they discuss their professors and sweethearts, arrange a serenade to a favorite teacher or a practical joke upon some sordid landlord or "philister;" they apostrophize Fatherland in patriotic speeches, pour out their hearts in a noisy flow of jolly good-fellowship, with pathos and pipes, lampoons and lager, sarcasm and sausages, shouts of laughter and song till midnight; like the uproarious crew in Auerbach's cellar. It must not be supposed, however, that all share in this boisterous mirth. The steady fellows live in almost ascetic retirement or seek friends of strict moral and literary habits.

"Providence has given to the French the empire of the land, to the English that of the sea, to the Germans that of the air. By this famous saying, Jean Paul, himself a denizen of the air, proclaimed the strength as well as the weakness of his native country; and those critics who in good or ill humor quote it to the disparagement of the Germans, seem to forget that the air is the habitation of the warbling nightingale and the soaring eagle, and is as necessary and useful to man as are the land and the sea; and situated as Germany is, in the heart of Europe, she furnishes the heart's blood, the ideas and principles of modern history and holds the intellectual mastery of the world."

As in times past, she produced the printing-press and the Reformation, the two levers of modern civilization and Christianity, so she reigns at the present day in every department of science and art, and these are, after all, next to virtue and religion, the noblest pursuits and the highest ornaments of immortal man.

In concluding this topic, permit me to say a few words on the transfer of German institutions of learning to American soil. What we need is:

1st. The obligatory education.

2d. More discipline in our schools.

3d. A thorough system of education in all branches.

It needs no argument to show that our college system is incomplete and that we need institutions of the first order, deserving the name of University in the full and proper sense of the term. The day is not distant when this great country will equal any on the globe in every branch of education.

As regards the organization of these future universities, however, we would by no means advocate a slavish copy of the German institutions, but such an adaptation of their features to the peculiar genius of our country, as will make them truly American and a real educational advance upon the old. It has been proposed already to establish such an institution in the city of New York; and it seems to me that we need at least one in every state and territory, to which the colleges will be preparatory like the German gymnasia. These universities ought to be planned on the largest scale, liberally endowed by the states and accessible to all. In these, our national system of education, which has so rapidly advanced of late, would find its necessary and natural completion. If the legislatures neglect this duty, the leading churches or private individuals should assume it. Such a movement would be more consistent with our national genius and would infuse a religious spirit into the institutions, without which they cannot permanently flourish and promote the highest interest of society.

A Course of Instruction.

1. *Primary Schools.*

The general outline of the eight years' course is nearly as follows :

I. First part, of two years, including children from six to eight years old ; four principal branches, namely :

1. Logical exercises, or oral teaching in the exercise of the powers of observation and expression, including religious instruction and the singing of hymns.

2. Elements of reading.

3. Elements of writing.

4. Elements of number, or arithmetic.

II. Second part, of two years, including children from eight to ten years old — seven principal branches, namely :

1. Exercises in reading.

2. Exercises in writing.

3. Religious and moral instruction, in select Bible narratives.

4. Language, or grammar.

5. Numbers, or arithmetic.

6. Doctrine of space and form, or geometry.

7. Singing by note, or elements of music.

III. Third part, of two years, including children from ten to twelve years old — eight principal branches, namely :

1. Exercises in reading and elocution.

2. Exercises in ornamental writing, preparatory to drawing.

3. Religious instruction in the connected Bible history.

4. Language, or grammar, with parsing.

5. Real instruction, or knowledge of nature and the external world, including the first elements of the sciences and the arts of life — of geography and history.

6. Arithmetic continued through fractions and the rules of proportion.

7. Geometry—doctrine of magnitudes and measures.

8. Singing and science of vocal and instrumental music.

IV. Fourth part, of two years, including children from ten to twelve years old — six principal branches, namely:

1. Religious instruction in the religious observation of nature; the life and discourses of Jesus Christ; the history of the Christian religion, in connection with the contemporary civil history; and the doctrines of Christianity.

2. Knowledge of the world, and of mankind, including civil society, elements of law, agriculture, mechanic arts, manufactures, etc.

3. Language, and exercises in composition.

4. Application of arithmetic and the mathematics to the business of life, including surveying and civil engineering.

5. Elements of drawing.

6. Exercises in singing, and the science of music.

V. Fifth part, of two years — children from twelve to fourteen.

1. Religious instruction, in the religious observation of nature, the life and discourses of Jesus Christ, the history of the Christian religion, in connection with the cotemporary civil history, and the principal doctrines of the Christian system.

The first topic of instruction mentioned under this head is one of peculiar interest and utility. The pupils are taught to observe, with care and system, the various powers and operations of nature, and to consider them as so many illustrations of the wisdom, power, and goodness of the Creator; and at each lesson they are directed to some appropriate passage of the Bible, which they read and commit to memory: and thus the idea is continually impressed on them, that the God of nature and the God of the Bible are one and the same Being.

For example, as introductory to the whole study, the first chapter of Genesis, together with some other appropriate passage of Scripture, as the 147th Psalm, or the 38th chapter of Job, may be read and committed to memory.

The surface of the earth, as illustrating the power and wisdom of God, may be taken as a lesson.

Then the varieties of surface, as mountains, valleys, oceans and rivers, continents and islands, the height of mountains, the breadth of oceans, the length of rivers, remarkable cataracts, extended caverns, volcanoes, tides, etc., may be taken into view, and the teacher may impress upon the class the greatness, power, and intelligence necessary for such a creation. The whole is fortified by the application of such a passage as Psalm civ, 1–13.

" Bless the Lord, O my soul! O Lord my God! thou art very great; thou art clothed with honor and majesty. Who coverest thyself with light as with a garment: who stretchest out the heavens like a curtain: who layeth the beams of his chambers in the waters : who maketh the clouds his chariot: who walketh upon the wings of the wind: who maketh his angels spirits; his ministers a flaming fire. Who laid the foundations of the earth, that it should not be removed forever. Thou coverest it with the deep as with a garment: the waters stood above the mountains. At thy rebuke they fled ; at the voice of thy thunder they hasted away. They go up by the mountains ; they go down by the valleys into the place which thou hast founded for them. Thou hast set a bound that they may not pass over ; that they turn not again to cover the earth. He sendeth the springs into the valleys, which run among the hills. They give drink to every beast of the field; the wild asses quench their thirst.

By them shall the fowls of the heaven have their habitation, which sing among the branches. He watereth the hills from his chambers : the earth is satisfied with the fruit of thy works."

" O Lord, how manifold are thy works ! in wisdom hast thou made them all : the earth is full of thy riches. So is this great and wide sea, wherein are things creeping innumerable, both small and great beasts. There go the ships : there is that leviathan, whom thou hast made to play therein."

The fruitfulness and beauty of the earth, as illustrating the wisdom and goodness of God, may serve as another lesson. Here may be exhibited the beauty and variety of the plants and flowers with which the earth is adorned ; the manner of their growth and self-propagation, their utility to man and beast, their immense number and variety, their relations to each other as genera and species; trees and their varieties, their beauty and utility, their timber and their fruit; and in connection with this lesson, Psalm civ, 14 – 34, may be committed to memory.

" He causeth the grass to grow for the cattle ; and herb for the service of man : that he may bring forth food out of the earth ; and wine that maketh glad the heart of man, and oil to make his face to shine, and bread which strengtheneth man's heart. The trees of the Lord are full of sap ; the cedars of Lebanon, which he hath planted ; where the birds make their nests : as for the stork, the fir trees are her house. The high hills are a refuge for the wild goats ; and the rocks for the conies. He appointeth the moon for seasons: the sun knoweth his going down. Thou maketh darkness, and it is night: wherein all the beasts of the forest do creep forth. The young lions roar after their prey, and seek their meat from God. The sun ariseth, they gather themselves together, and lay them down in their dens. Man goeth forth unto his work and to his labor until the evening."

" These wait all upon thee ; that thou mayest give them their meat in due season. That thou givest them they gather ; thou openest thine hand, they are filled with good. Thou hidest thy face, they are troubled : thou takest away their breath, they die, and return to their dust. Thou sendest forth thy Spirit, they are created :

and thou renewest the face of the earth. The glory of the Lord shall endure forever; the Lord shall rejoice in his works. He looketh on the earth, and it trembleth : he toucheth the hills, and they smoke. I will sing unto the Lord as long as I live : I will sing praise to my God while I have my being. My meditation of him shall be sweet : I will be glad in the Lord."

In like manner, the creation and nourishment, the habits and instincts of various animals may be contemplated, in connection with Proverbs, vi, 6 – 8; Psalm civ, 17–22; Proverbs, xxx, 24 – 31; Gen. i, 20 – 24; Psalm cxlv, 15–16.

"Go to the ant, thou sluggard ! consider her ways, and be wise : Which having no guide, overseer, or ruler, provideth her meat in the summer, and gathereth her food in the harvest."

" There be four things which are little on the earth, but they are exceeding wise : the ants are a people not strong, yet they prepare their meat in the summer; the conies are but a feeble folk, yet make they their houses in the rocks ; the locusts have no king, yet go they forth all of them by bands ; the spider taketh hold with her hands, and is in king's palaces. There be three things which go well, yea, four are comely in going : a lion, which is strongest among beasts, and turneth not away for any : a greyhound ; a he-goat also ; and a king, against whom there is no rising up."

" And God said, Let the earth bring forth the living creature after his kind, cattle, and creeping thing, and beasts of the earth after his kind : and it was so. And God made the beasts of the earth after his kind, and cattle after their kind, and everything that creepeth upon the earth after his kind : and God saw that it was good."

" The eyes of all wait upon thee : and thou givest them their meat in due season. Thou openest thine hand, and satisfiest the desire of every living thing. The Lord is righteous in all his ways, and holy in all his works."

The phenomena of light and color, the nature of the rainbow, etc., may make another interesting lesson, illustrating the unknown forms of beauty and glory which exist in the Divine mind, and which he may yet develop in other and still more glorious worlds; in connection with Gen., i, 3, 5, 9, 13, 14, and other passages of like kind.

So the properties of the air, wind, and storm, Job, xxviii, 25; xxxviii, 33, 34, 35; Psalm cxlviii, 8.

"Knowest thou the ordinance of heaven? canst thou set the dominion thereof in the earth? Canst thou lift up thy voice to the clouds, that abundance of waters may cover thee? Canst thou send lightnings, that they may go, and say unto thee, Here we are? Who hath put wisdom in the inward parts? or who hath given understanding to the heart? Who can number the clouds in wisdom? or who can stay the battles of heaven?"

Then the heavens, the sun, moon, planets, fixed stars, and comets, the whole science of astronomy, so far as it can be introduced with advantage into common schools, can be contemplated in the same way. The enlightening, elevating, and purifing moral influence of such a scheme of instruction, carried through the whole system of nature, must be clearly obvious to every thinking mind; and its utility, considered merely with reference to worldly good, is no less manifest. The second topic of religious instruction is more exclusively scriptural. The life of Christ, and the history of the apostles, as given in the New Testament, are chronologically arranged, and tables formed as before. (III, 3.) The discourses of Christ are examined and explained in their chronological arrangement, and in the same way the discourses and epistles of the apostles. The history of Christianity, in connection with the cotemporary civil history, is taught in a series of conversational lectures. To conclude the whole course of religious instruction, a summary of the Christian doctrine is given in the form of some approved catechism.

2. Knowledge of the world and of mankind, including civil society, constitutional law, agriculture, mechanic arts, manufactures, etc.

This is a continuation and completion, in a more systematic form, of the instruction commenced in III, 5. The course begins with the family, and the first object is to construct a habitation. The pupil tells what materials are necessary for this purpose, where they are to be found, how brought together and fitted into the several parts of the building. The house must now be furnished. The different articles of furniture and their uses are named in systematic order, the materials of which they are made, and the various trades employed in making them are enumerated. Then comes the garden, its tools and products, and whatever else is necessary for the subsistence and physical comfort of a family. Then the family duties and virtues; parental and filial obligation and affection; rights of property: duties of neighborhoods; the civil relations of society; the religious relations of society; the state, the father-land, etc.; finally, geography, history, and travels. Books of travels are compiled expressly for the use of schools, and are found to be of the highest interest and utility.

3. Language, and exercises in composition.

The object here is to give the pupils a perfect command of their native tongue, and ability to use it on all occasions with readiness and power. The first exercises are on simple questions, such as, "Why ought children to love and obey their parents?" or they are short descriptions of visible objects, such as a house, a room, a garden, etc. There are also exercises on the various forms of expressing the same idea, as, "The sun enlightens the earth." "The earth is enlightened by the sun." "The sun gives light to the earth." "The earth receives light from the sun." "The sun is the source of light to the earth." "The sun sends out its rays to enlighten the earth." "The earth is enlightened by rays sent out from the sun," etc. There are exercises also of the same sort on metaphors and other figures of speech. Familiar letters are then written, and short essays on themes such as may be furnished by texts from the Book of Proverbs, and other sentences of the kind; and thus gradual advancement is made to all the higher and graver modes of composition.

4. Application of arithmetic and the mathematics to the business of life, including surveying, civil engineering, etc.

The utility of this branch of instruction, and the mode of it, after what has already been said, are probably too obvious to need any further illustration.

5. Elements of drawing.

For this the pupils have already been prepared by the exercises in ornamental writing, in the previous part of the course. They have already acquired that accuracy of sight and steadiness of hand which are among the most essential requisites to drawing well. The first exercises are in drawing lines, and the most simple mathematical figures, such as the square, the cube, the triangle, the parallelogram; generally from wooden models, placed at some little distance on a shelf, before the class. From this they proceed to architectural figures, such as doors, windows, columns, facades. Then the figures of animals, such as a horse, a cow, an elephant; first from other pictures, and then from nature. A plant, a rose, or some flower is placed upon a shelf, and the class make a picture of it.

From this they proceed to landscape painting, historical painting and the higher branches of the art, according to their time and capacity. All learn enough of drawing to use it in the common business of life, such as plotting a field, laying out a canal, or drawing the plan of a building; and many attain to a high degree of excellence.

6. Exercises in singing and the science of music.

The instructions of the previous parts are extended as far as possible, and include singing and playing at sight, and the more abstruse and difficult branches of the science and art of music.

In Bavaria, Wirtemburg, the Duchy of Baden and Nassau, as much, and in Wirtemburg and Baden, perhaps even more, has been done to promote the intelligence, morality, and civilization of the lower orders of society, than in Prussia. In each of these countries, every village has a good school-house, and at least one learned and practically efficient teacher, who has been educated for several years at a college; every town has several well-organized schools, sufficiently large to receive all the children of the town, who are between the ages of six and fourteen; each of these schools contains from four to ten class-rooms, and each class-room is under the direction of a highly educated teacher.

In each of these countries, every parent is obliged to educate his children, either at home or at some school, the choice of means being left to himself. In none of these countries are children left to grow up in vicious ignorance or with debasing habits.

In none of these countries, is there any class of children analogous to that which swarms in the back streets, alleys and gutters of our great cities and towns, and from which, our paupers, our disaffected, and our criminals grow up, and from which our " ragged schools " are filled. All the children are intelligent, polite, clean, and neatly dressed, and grow up from their sixth to their fourteenth year under the teaching and influence of educated men.

In each of these countries a sufficient number of normal colleges has been founded, to enable it to educate a sufficient supply of teachers for the parishes and towns.

In each of these countries, all the schools of every sect and party, private as well as public, are open to public inspection, and are visited several times every year by learned men, whose business it is to examine both teachers and scholars, and to give the government, the chambers, and the country, a full and detailed account of the state, condition, character, and progress of every school, so that parents may know where to send their children with safety ; that good teachers may be encouraged, rewarded, and promoted ; and that unworthy teachers may not be suffered to continue long in their situations.

In each of these countries, the laws prohibit any person being a teacher of any school, until he has proved his efficiency to the committee of professors, appointed by the state to examine candidates, and until he has laid before such committee testimonials of character from his religious minister, his neighbors, and the professors of the college at which he was educated.

2. *Burger or Middle Schools.*

RELIGIOUS INSTRUCTION.

Class VI. Four hours per week. Narration by the teacher of stories from the Old Testament, in the words of the Bible, repeated by the pupils. Easy verses learned by heart.

Class V. Four hours. Stories from the gospels, except the latter portion of the life of Christ. Church songs and Bible verses learned.

Class IV. Three hours. The Old Testament in a more connected form. The moral of the history is impressed upon the children. The Ten Commandments and church songs committed to memory.

Class III. Two hours. The life and doctrines of Christ, to the period of his imprisonment. Church history. Four weeks are set apart for learning the geography of Palestine.

Class II. Two hours. The Protestant catechism committed to memory and explained. Church songs and verses committed.

Class I. Two hours. A compendium of the history of the Christian Church, particularly after the apostolic age. History of the Reformation. Review of the Bible. Committing to memory psalms and hymns continued.

GERMAN LANGUAGE.

Class VI. Four hours. Exercises of speech. Stories narrated to the children and repeated by them. After learning to write, these stories are written upon the slate.

Class V. Four hours. Exercises in orthography. Etymology begun.

Class IV. Four hours. Exercises in orthography and style.. Every week a short composition is written on some subject which has been narrated.

Class III. Grammar continued.

Class II. Four hours. Original compositions, which are corrected during the recitations. Syntax commenced.

Class I. Three hours. Compositions on historical subjects. Essays written at home, and corrected in the classroom. Syntax continued.

LATIN LANGUAGE.

Class IV. Three hours. Declensions of nouns, adjectives, and pronouns learned. Examples learned by heart, and others written as an exercise at home. Auxiliary verbs conjugated.

Class III. Four hours. Comparison of adjectives. Regular verbs conjugated.

Class II. Four hours. Irregular verbs. Syntax begun. Translation from Latin into German.

Class I. Six hours. Grammar continued. Written exercises at home and in the class. Every four weeks an extempore exercise is written, which the teachers correct out of school hours. Cornelius Nepos read and construed.

FRENCH LANGUAGE.

Class III. Three hours. Exercises in reading. Elements of grammar. Words learned by heart. Easy exercises written at home and in school hours.

Class II. Four hours. Regular and irregular verbs learned. Syntax. Translations from French into German. Words learned by rote.

Class I. Four hours. Written exercises of increased difficulty. Tables dictated and learned by heart. Voltaire's Charles XII read.

ARITHMETIC.

Class VI. Four hours. Practical arithmetic. The fundamental operations taught with numbers from one to one hundred; first mentally, then with blocks, and afterward with figures. Exercises prepared at home twice a week.

Class V. Four hours. The four ground rules continued, with numbers as high as one thousand. Exercises in reading and writing large numbers. Mental arithmetic especially practiced. Addition and subtraction of abstract numbers.

Class IV. Four hours. Addition and subtraction revised. Multiplication and division of abstract numbers. Weights and measures explained.

Class III. Four hours. The four ground rules with fractions.

Class II. Three hours. Revision of the above. Rule of three.

Class I. Three hours. In the first year practical arithmetic finished. Proportions and decimal fractions. Elements of algebra. Mental algebra.

GEOMETRY.

Class IV. Two hours. The essential preparatory exercises in form, in connection with drawing. Rudiments explained.

Class III. Two hours. Practice in the position of points, drawing of lines, angles, plane figures, representations of solids.

Class II. Two hours. Elements of geometry proper, the point, line, angles, triangles, and measures of straight lines, surfaces, and contents.

Class I. Two hours. Plane geometry completed, with practical exercises. Every alternate six months, lessons in physics are given.

NATURAL HISTORY.

Class II. Two hours. In the summer term, study of certain classes of plants. In the winter term, of animals. The subject is illustrated by drawings.

Class I. Two hours. Systematic botany during the winter term, and zoology and mineralogy during the winter.

GEOGRAPHY.

Class III. Two hours. Knowledge of home. Berlin and its environs. Regency of Potsdam. Province of Brandenburg. Necessary technical terms explained, as horizontal, vertical, etc.

Class II. Two hours. Geography of Prussia and Germany.

Class I. Two hours. General geography, particularly Europe and America. Asia more generally, Africa and Australia very briefly.

HISTORY.

Class II. Two hours. View of universal history, biographical rather than chronological.

Class I. Two hours. First year universal history completed. Second year the history of Germany, and particularly of Prussia. The most important inventions and discoveries are noticed in connection with the history of these countries.

READING.

Class VI. Seven hours. Reading by the phonic (lautir) method. Analysis of words in regard to division into syllables and sounds.

Class V. Seven hours. Mechanical reading continued, but with reference to the meaning of the words. The pupils are examined upon words, sentences, and paragraphs.

Class IV. Four hours. Explanatory reading continued Accentuation. No piece is allowed to be read without it being understood.

Class III. Two hours. Rythmical reading begun. Interesting portions of the matter read, narrated by the pupils in their own words.

Class II. Two hours. Rythmical reading continued.

Class I. Two hours. Reading of some of the German classics. Analysis of the subject read.

WRITING.

Class VI. Five hours. Introductory exercises of drawing upon the slate. Copying the small letters from the blackboard. Writing on paper. Capital letters. Written exercises at home twice a week.

Class V. Five hours. Writing of German characters continued. Roman letters begun. Copying from a book at home, with special reference to orthography.

Class IV. Four hours. Writing in German and Roman characters continued. Two hours copying from copy-slips. Two hours writing from dictation.

Class III. Three hours. Exercises of Class IV, continued. Pupils who write well are allowed to write without lines. Writing without copies, according to progress.

Class II. Two hours. Exercises continued. Most of the pupils write without lines, or by directing points merely.

Class I. The written exercises in other departments are examined, to ascertain the character of the handwriting. No special lessons are given.

DRAWING.

Class IV. Two hours. Drawing straight lines in various directions and of various lengths. Making definite angles. Drawing triangles, squares, and other rectilinear figures.

Class III. Two hours. Drawing of circles and ovals.

Class II. Two hours. Drawing of bodies bounded by planes and straight lines in perspective. Drawing of curves.

Class I. Drawing from natural objects, from plaster casts and models.

SINGING.

Class IV. Two hours suffice to learn fifteen or twenty songs, of one or two verses, by note, and some ten choral songs.

Class III. Two hours. Songs with two parts continued. Chorals with one voice.

Class II. Two hours. Songs with two or three voices continued.

Class I. Two hours. Songs and chorals with three or four parts.

Once during the morning there is an interval for recreation in the court-yard of the school, and the pupils are directed in their exercises of marching and counter-marching, and the like, by one of the teachers.

The course marked out in the foregoing programme, as far as it extends, seems to me well adapted to educate the moral and intellectual faculties, as well as the senses; to give mental vigor, while it furnishes information useful to the pupil in after life.

3. *Teacher's Seminary.*

The following table will show what the subjects of instruction are :

TIME TABLE IN TEACHERS' COLLEGE IN DRESDEN.

Summer Half Year.			Winter Half Year.			
Number of hours each Week in Class.			Number of hours each Week in Class.			CLASSES.
I.	II.	III.	I.	II.	III.	
2	2	2	2	2	2	1. Religion.
0	1	1	2	1	1	2. Explanation of the Scriptures.
0	1	1	0	1	1	3. Scripture history.
3	1	1	3	0	0	4. Catechism.
1	0	0	1	0	0	5. Religious exhortation.
2	0	0	2	0	0	6. Pedagogy.
0	3	3	0	3	3	7. Special methods of teaching.
2	1	1	2	0	0	{ 8. I. Rhetoric and reading exercises ; II and III. Mental calculations.
1	1	1	1	1	1	9. Recitation.
2	0	0	2	0	0	10. Natural philosophy.
0	2	2	0	2	2	11. Natural history.
0	1	1	0	1	1	12. Geography.
1	0	0	0	0	0	13. Mathematical geography.
1	1	1	1	1	1	14. History.
1	2	2	1	2	2	15. German language.
2	0	0	2	0	·0	16. Latin language.
2	2	2	2	2	2	17. Writing.
?	2	1	2	2	2	18. Arithmetic.
0	1	2	0	0	· 0	19. Geometrical drawing.
1	0	0	1	1	1	20. Geometry.
2	2	2	2	2	2	21. Drawing.
0	0	1	1	1	2	22. Singing.
1	1	1	1	1	1	23. Choral singing.
1	1	0	0	0	0	24. Quartet singing.
2	2	2	2	2	2	25. Concert singing.
6	3	2	3	1	6	{ 26. I. Organ playing. II and III. Violin playing.
13	19	19	7	12	6	27. Preparation and exercise hours.
2	2	2	2	2	2	28. Gymnastic exercises.
52	51	50	42	40	40	Total number of hours per week.

The students rise in summer at 5 o'clock, and in winter at 6 o'clock, in the morning: as soon as they are dressed, they meet in one of the class-rooms, where the director reads the morning prayers; their hours of study are from 7 to 12 A. M. and from 2 to 5 P.M.

Connected with the college is a primary school for children of that district of the city, in which the college is situated: this school is under the direction of a regularly appointed and experienced teacher, and is attended by 105 children, who are divided into three classes, to each of which is assigned a separate class-room in one part of the college buildings. In these classes, a certain number of students from the college first practice teaching under the eye, and aided by the advice of the teacher.

At the end of this long and careful preparation, they are called before the board of examiners. If the young man is a Protestant, his religious examination is conducted by the board of examiners themselves; but if he is a Romanist, a priest is joined to the board, and conducts the religious part of the examination.

The examination lasts three days. On the first day the subjects are —

From 1 to 10 o'clock, A. M., Scripture history.
  " 10 to 12   "   "   Pedagogy.
  " 2 to 4   "   P. M., Mathematics and the theory of music.

The answers to the questions of the first day's examination are given in writing. On the second day the subjects are—

From 7 to 11 o'clock, A. M., { Catechising a class of village school children on some subject of elementary instruction.

  " 11 to 12   "   " { Reading; Arithmetic; and An object lesson given to school children.

From 1 to 2 o'clock P. M.,

{ A *vivâ voce* examination—
In religion ;
The Scriptures ;
Luther's catechism ; and
Pedagogy.

" 4 to 5 " "

{ German language ;
Logic ; and
Psychology.

" 5 to 6 " "

{ History ;
Geography ;
Natural philosophy ; and
Natural history.

On the third day the subjects of examination are —

Organ playing ;
Singing ;
Piano-forte ; and
Violin.

If the young candidate, who had been educated for four years in a teachers' college, can not pass this examination so as to satisfy the examiners, he is obliged to continue his studies until he can do so. But if he passes the examination in a satisfactory manner, the examiners grant him a diploma, which is marked " excellent," " good," or " passable," according to the manner in which he acquitted himself in his examination.

If the young candidate does not obtain a certificate marked " excellent," but only one marked " good," or " passable," he can not officiate as teacher, until he has spent two years in some school as assistant to an experienced teacher.

At the end of this time, he is obliged again to present himself to the board of examiners, who examine him again in the most careful and searching manner. If he passes this examination, he receives another diploma marked " excellent," " good," or " passable," according to his merit, and if he obtains a diploma marked " excellent," he is enrolled among the members of the teachers' profession, and is allowed to officiate either as a private tutor or as a village teacher. But if he can not obtain this diploma, he is obliged to continue to act as an assistant teacher until he can do so. Seminar Director Dr. Otto, the principal of the normal college, and a member of the board of examiners, assured me, that it was a common thing for candidates to be examined four or five times, before they succeeded in obtaining a teachers' diploma. When they have at last succeeded, they, as well as those who obtained the diploma marked " excellent " in the first examination, are eligible as teachers.

The school committee of the different parishes elect their own teachers. The only condition, to which this right is subjected is, that they may not elect any person, who has not obtained a diploma of competence from the board of examiners.

4. *City Trade School.*

The City Trade School is to give a more appropriate education for the mechanic arts and higher trades then can be had through the courses of classical schools. It is a great point gained, when the principle is admitted that different kinds of education are suited to different objects in life ; and such an admission belongs to an advanced stage of education. As a consequence of a general sentiment of this kind, numerous schools for the appropriate instruction of those not intended for the learned professions grow up by the side of the others.

THIRD CLASS.

Physics. Electricity and magnetism, with experiments. Two hours. Chemistry. Water and non-metallic bodies with experiments. Two hours.

Writing. Two hours. Architectural and topographical drawing. Two hours. Some of the pupils during this time are engaged in ornamental drawing.

Vocal music. Two hours.

SECOND CLASS.

Religious Instruction. Explanation of the first three gospels. History of the Christian religion and church to the reformation. Two hours.

German. Correction of exercises written at home, upon subjects assigned by the teacher. Oral and written exercises. Introduction to the history of German poetry. Three hours.

French. Grammar; extemporalia for the application of the rules. Written and oral translations from German into French, from Beauvais's Manual, and vice versa, from Ideler and Nolte's Manual. Four hours.

English. Exercises in reading and speaking. Translation into German, from Burkhardt. Dictation. Verbs. Two hours.

Arithmetic. Commercial Arithmetic. Algebra, to include simple and quadratic equations. Logarithyms. Three hours.

Geometry. Circles. Analytical and plane trigonometry. Three hours.

Geography. The states of Europe, with special reference to their population, manufactures and commerce. Two hours.

History. Principal events of the history of the middle ages and of later times, as an introduction to recent history. One hour.

Natural History. Mineralogy. Physiology of plants. Three hours.

Chemistry. Metallic bodies and their compounds, with experiments. Three hours.

Architectural, topographical, and plain drawing. Drawing with instruments. Introduction to India ink drawing. Beginning of the science of construction. Two hours.

Drawing. From copies, and from plaster and other models. Two hours. This kind of drawing may be learned instead of the above.

Vocal music. Two hours.

First Class.

Religious Instruction. History of the Christian religion and church continued. References to the Bible. One hour.

German. History of German literature to recent times. Essays. Exercises of delivery. Three hours.

French. Reading from the manual of Buchner and Hermunn, with abstracts. Classic authors read. Review of grammar. Exercises at home, and extemporalia. Free delivery. Correction of exercises. Four hours.

English. Syntax, with written and extempore exercises from Burkhardt. Reading of classic authors. Writing of letters. Exercises in speaking.

Arithmetic. Algebra. Simple and quadratic equations. Binomial and polynomial theorems. Higher equations. Commercial arithmetic continued. Three hours.

Geometry. Plane trigonometry and its applications. Conic sections. Descriptive geometry. Three hours.

History. History of the middle ages. Modern history with special reference to the progress of civilization, of inventions, discoveries, and of commerce and industry. Three hours.

Natural History. In summer, botany, the principal families, according to the natural system. In winter, zoology. The pupils are taken, for the purpose of examining specimens, to the Royal Museum.

Physics. In summer, optics with experiments. In winter, the system of the world. Three hours.

Technology. Chemical and mechanical arts and trades, described and illustrating by models. Excursions to visit the principal workshops. Four hours.

Architectural and machine drawing. Two hours. those pupils who do not take part in this, receive lessons in ornamental drawing from plaster models.

Vocal music. Two hours.

The pupils of this class are, besides, engaged in manipulating in the laboratory of the institution several hours each week.

The facilities for the courses are furnished by a collection of mathematical and physical apparatus, a laboratory, with a tolerably complete chemical apparatus and a series of tests, a collection of specimens of the arts and manufactures (or technological collection) a collection of dried plants, and of engravings for the botanical course, and a small garden for the same use, a collection of minerals, a collection of insects, a collection in comparative anatomy, a series of engravings for the drawing course, and of plaster models, a set of maps, and other apparatus for geography, some astronomical instruments, and a library. The pupils are taken from time to time, to the admirable museum attached to the university of Berlin, for the examination of zoological specimens especially.

5. *Royal Real Schools.*

The Royal Real School of Berlin was founded as early as 1747, by Counsellor Hecker. At the period in which this school was founded, Latin and Greek were the exclusive objects of study in the learned schools, and the avowed purpose of this establishment was that " not mere words should be taught to the pupils, but realities, explanations being made to them from nature, from models and plans, and from subjects calculated to be useful in after-life." Hence the school was called a "real school," and preserves this name, indicative of the great educational reform which it was intended to promote, and the success of which has been, though slow, most certain.

In the Royal Real School the branches of instruction are — religion, Latin, French, English, German, physics, natural history, chemistry, history, geography, drawing, writing, and vocal music. The Latin is retained as practically useful in some branches of trade, as in pharmacy, as aiding in the nomenclature of natural history, and as preventing a separation in the classes of this school and that of the gymnasium, which would debar the pupils from passing from the former to the latter in the upper classes. It must be admitted that, for all purposes but the last, it occupies an unnecessary degree of attention, especially in the middle classes.

The following table shows the distribution of time among the courses. There are seven classes in numerical order, but ten, in fact, the third, fourth, and fifth being divided into two; the lower fourth is again, on account of its numbers, subdivided into two parallel sectious. Of these the seventh, sixth, and fifth are elementary classes, the pupils entering the seventh at between five and seven years of age. In the annexed table the number. of hours of recitation per week of each class in the several subjects is stated, and the vertical column separating the elementary classes from the others, contains the sum of the hours devoted to each branch in the higher clases, excluding the lower section of the fourth class, which has not a distinct course from that of the other division.

TABLE SHOWING THE NUMBER OF HOURS OF RECITATION PER WEEK, OF EACH CLASS, IN THE SUBJECTS TAUGHT IN THE ROYAL REAL SCHOOL OF BERLIN.

SUBJECTS of STUDY.	First Class.	Second Class.	Third Class, A.	Third Class, B.	Fourth Class, A.	Fourth Class, B. I.	Fourth Class, B. II.	Sum of the hours in the seven upper classes.	Fifth Class, A.	Fifth Class, B.	Sixth Class.	Seventh Class.	Proportion of other studies to German in the — Royal Real School.	First six classes of the Freder'k Wm. Gymn.	In all the classes of the Freder'k Wm. Gymn.
Latin,...........	4	4	4	5	6	5	6	28					1.4	2.9	3
French,.........	4	4	4	3	3	4	4	22	4	5			1.1	0.7	0.9
English,........	2	2	2					6					0.3		
German,........	3	3	3	4	3	4	4	20	8	8	10	10	1.0	0.8	1.0
Religion,........	2	2	2	2	2	2	2	12	2	3	2	2	0.6	0.6	0.8
Mathematics,*...	6	6	5	6	7	6	4	35	4	3	6	6	1.7	1.1	1.6
Natural History,..	3	2	2	2				9					0.4	0.1†	0.1
Physics,.........	2	2	2	2				8					0.4	0.2†	0.2
Chemistry,.......	2	2	2	2				8					0.4		
Geography,......					3	3	3	9	2	2	2		0.4	0.5	0.5
History,.........	3	3	3	2	2	2	2	15	2	2	2		0.7	0.3	0.7
Drawing,........	2	2	2	2	2	2	2	12					0.6	0.4	0.4
Writing,........					2	2	2	4	4	4	6	8	0.2	0.3	0.3
Singing,.........	2	4	3	2	2	2	2	15					0.7	0.6	0.6
Total,....	36	36	35	35	32	32	32		26	26	26	26			

Pupils who enter this school between five and seven years of age, and go regularly through the elementary classes, are prepared at ten to pass to its higher classes, or to enter the lowest of the gymnasium. It is thus after the fifth class that a comparison of the two institutions must begin. The studies of the real school proper, and of the gymnasium, have exactly the same elementary basis, and they remain so far parallel to each other that a pupil, by taking extra instruction in Greek, may pass from the lower third class of the former to the lower third of the latter. This fact alone is sufficient to show that the real

* Including arithmetic, geometry, and trigonometry.

† These numbers include the entire course.

schools must be institutions for secondary instruction, since the pupils have yet three classes to pass through after reaching the point just referred to. It serves also to separate the real schools from the higher burgher schools, since the extreme limit of the courses of the latter, with the same assistance in regard to Greek, only enables the pupil to reach the lower third class of the gymnasium. In general, a pupil would terminate his studies in the real school at between sixteen and eighteen years of age. The difference between the subjects of instruction in the real school and the Frederick William gymnasium, consists in the omission in the former of Greek, Hebrew, and philosophy, and the introduction of English and chemistry. The relative proportions of time occupied in the same subjects in the two schools, will be seen by comparing the two columns next on the right of the numbers for the seventh class, in the table just given. The first of these columns contains the proportion of the number of hours per week devoted to the different subjects in the six classes of the real school above the elementary, the number of hours devoted to the German being taken as unity; and the second, the same proportion for six classes of the gymnasium, beginning with the lowest, the same number of hours being taken as the unit, as in the preceding column.

6. *Frederick William Gymnasium of Berlin.*

The numbers attached to the names of the different classes, in the following programme, show the number of hours of study per week in the regular branches in which the division of classes takes place. In like manner, the numbers attached to the several subjects of study show how many hours are occupied per week in each of the subjects by the several classes.

Sixth Class, Thirty Hours.

Latin. Inflections of nouns, etc. Comparisons. Conjugation of the indicative moods of regular and of some irregular verbs. Translation from Blume's elementary book. Exercises from Blume. Extemporalia. Ten hours.

German. Etymology and syntax. Exercises in writing upon subjects previously narrated. Exercises in orthography, reading and declaiming. Four hours.

French. Etymology, to include the auxiliary verbs, in Herrmann's grammar. Oral and written exercises. Reading and translation. Exercises on the rules from the grammar. Three hours.

Religion. Bible history of the Old Testament. Committing to memory selected verses. Two hours.

Geography. Delineation of the outlines of Europe, Africa, Asia, and America, from determinate points given. Divisions of the countries, with their principal cities, rivers and mountains. Two hours.

Arithmetic. The four ground rules, with denominate whole numbers. Their applications. Four hours.

Writing. Elements of round and running hand. Dictation. Writing from copy slips. Three hours.

Drawing. Exercises in drawing lines. Two hours.

Fifth Class, Twenty-Nine Hours.

Latin. Etymology. Use of the prepositions. The accusative before an infinitive, practiced orally and in writing, and extempore, and in exercises. Translation from Blume's reader. Ten hours.

German. Parsing, reading and declamation. Exercises on narrations. Four hours. French. Etymology, by oral and written exercises. Easier stories from Hermann's reader. Three hours.

Religion. Explanation of the gospels, according to St. Matthew and St. Luke. Committing to memory the principal facts. Two hours. Geography. Review of the last year's course. Rivers and mountains of Europe, and chief towns, in connection. Two hours.

Arithmetic. Review of the preceding. Fractions. Four hours.

Writing. Running hand from copy slips. Two hours.

Drawing. Drawing from bodies, terminated by planes and straight lines. Two hours.

FOURTH CLASS, TWENTY-EIGHT HOURS.

Latin. Review of etymology. The principal rules enforced by oral and written exercises and extemporalia. Translation from Jacob's reader and Corn. Nepos. Ten hours.

German. Compositions on subjects previously read. Declamation. Reading from Kalisch's reader. Parsing. Three hours.

French. Review of etymology. Irregular verbs. Reciprocal verbs. Anecdotes and narrations from Hermann's grammar, and committing the principal to memory. Two hours.

Religion. Gospel according to St. Matthew, explained. Verses and psalms committed to memory. Two hours.

Geography. Political geography of Germany, and of the rest of Europe. Review of the geography of the other parts of the world. Three hours.

Arithmetic. Review of fractions. Simple and compound proportion. Partnership. Simple interest. Three hours.

Geometry. Knowledge of forms, treated inductively. One hour.

Writing. Running hand, from copy slips. Two hours.

Drawing. From bodies bounded by curved lines. Two hours.

LOWER THIRD CLASS, THIRTY HOURS.

Latin. Syntax. Rules of cases from Zumpt. Exercises and extemporalia. Inflections formerly learned reviewed. Cornelius Nepos. Eight hours.

Greek. Etymology, from Buttmann's grammar to regular verbs, included. Translations from Greek into German from Jacob's, from German into Greek from Hess's exercises. Six hours.

German. Compositions in narration and description. Declamation. Two hours.

French. Repetition of inflections, and exercises by extemporalia and in writing. Translation of the fables from Herrmann's reading book, 2d course. Two hours.

Religion. Morals, and Christian faith. Two hours.

Geography. Physical geography. Europe and the other parts of the world. Two hours.

History. General view of ancient and modern history. Two hours.

Mathematics. Legendre's geometry, book 1. Decimals. Algebra. Square and cube root. Four hours.

Drawing. Introduction to landscape drawing. Two hours.

UPPER THIRD CLASS, THIRTY HOURS.

Latin. Division 1. Syntax, from Zumpt. Review of the preceding course. Oral exercises in construction of sentences. Written exercises and extemporalia. Cæsar Bell. Gall., books 1, 2, and 7, in part. Ovid's Metamorphoses, extracts from books 7 and 8. Prosody, rules from Zumpt. Ten hours.

Greek. Division 1. Etymology, from Buttmann's grammar. Oral and written exercises and extemporalia. Jacob's reader. Six hours.

German. Examination of exercises on historical subjects. Poetical selections for declamation. Two hours.

French. Exercises in translation. Written exercises. Extemporalia. Two hours.

Religion. Principal passages from the gospels gone over. General view of the Old Testament writings. Two hours.

History and Geography. Roman history from the Punic Wars to the destruction of the western empire. History of the middle ages, three hours. Review of the five general divisions of the world, one hour. Four hours.

Mathematics. Geometry. Legendre, books 1 and 2, and part of 3. Algebra, with exercises from Meyer Hirsch. Four hours.

LOWER SECOND CLASS, THIRTY-ONE HOURS.

Latin. Extracts from Livy and Cæsar de Bell. Civ. Review of Bell. Gall., books 2 and 3. Syntax. Exercises and extemporalia. Committing to memory exercises from Livy and Cæsar. Ovid's Metamophoses, books 11 to 14. Eight hours.

Greek. Homer's Odys., 11 12, 13, and 14. Exercises on the dialects. Xenophon's Anab., 1, 2, and, part of 3. Excerpts from the grammar reviewed. Exercises and extemporalia. Syntax. Six hours.

Hebrew. Grammar, ending with irregular verbs. Easier parts of historical books of Scripture translated. Vocabulary learned by rote. Exercises on regular and irregular verbs out of the recitation room. Two hours.

German. Correction of written exercises and essays. Exercises on delivery. Two hours.

French. Voltaire's Charles XII. Exercises and extemporalia. Two hours.

Religion. Explanation of the principal parts of the Epistles of St. Paul, with historical sketches, and a view of the life of early Christian communities. Two hours.

History. Roman history, from the Punic Wars. History of the middle ages concluded. General view of history. Three hours.

Mathematics. Geometry to proportions and simple figures. Elements of algebra. Logarithms. Four hours. Natural History. Mineralogy. Botany, especially of native plants. Two hours.

UPPER SECOND CLASS, THIRTY-TWO HOURS.

Latin. Cicero's Orations, pro. Rosc. Amer., de Amic., de Senectute. Livy, books 22 to 25, inclusive. Virgil's Æneid, books 1 and 2. Some eclogues and excerpts from Georgics. Exercises and extemporalia. Nine hours.

Greek. Homer's Iliad, books 4 to 11, inclusive. Arrian Alex. expedition, books 1 and 2. Buttmann's grammar with exercises and extemporalia. Six hours.

Hebrew. Books of Judges and of Ruth, with exercises of syntax. Easy exercises, and committing vocabulary to memory out of the class-room. Two hours.

German. Essays. Delivery. Two hours.

French. Excerpts from Harmann and Brüchner's manual of the more recent French literature. Two hours.

Religion. Christian faith and morals. Two hours.

History. Review of ancient history and geography, using the Latin language. Three hours.

Mathematics. Arithmetical geometry and plane trigonometry. Algebraic exercises. Polygons. Stereometry. Simple and quadratic equations. Four hours.

Physics. General physics. Electricity and magnetism. Two hours.

FIRST CLASS, THIRTY-ONE HOURS.

Latin. Horace's Odes, books 3 and 4. Cicero against Verres. Tacitus Annals, books 11 and 12, and extracts from 3 to 6. Cicero, Tusc. quest. Extempore translations from German into Latin. Exercises. Declamation. Eight hours.

Greek. Homer's Iliad, book 16, Odyssey, books 9 to 16, inclusive. Hippias Major, Charmides and Gorsias of Plato, (excerpts.) Sophocles' Edip. tyr. and Antigone. Grammatical exercises. Buttmann's grammar. Six hours.

Hebrew. Second book of Kings. Genesis. Psalms, 16 to 100. Grammatical criticisms of historical excerpts, or of psalms, as an exercise at home. Two hours.

German. Criticism of compositions. General grammar, and history of the German grammar and literature. One hour.

French. Selections from Scribe and Delavigne. Exercises and extemporalia. Two hours.

Religion. History of the Christian church, to the times of Gregory VII. Two hours.

History. Modern history, and review. Three hours.

Mathematics. Plane trigonometry and application of algebra to geometry. Algebra. Mensuration and conic sections. Binomial theorem. Exponential and trigon. functions. Four hours.

Physics. Physical geography. Mechanics. Two hours.

Philosophy. Propædeutics. Logic. One hour.

There are five classes for vocal music, the fifth receiving two hours of instruction in musical notation and singing by ear. The fourth, time and cliffs, etc. Exercises in the natural scale and harmony. Songs and chorals with one part. The third, two hours formation of the scale of sharps, running the gamut with difficult intervals, combined with the practical exercises of the last class. The second, two hours, repetition of tones; sharps, and flats. Formation of the scale of flats. Exercises of songs and chorals, in two parts. The first class is an application of what has been learned, as well as a continuation of the science and art, and all the pupils do not, of course, take part in this stage of the instruction. The course is of four hours per week, two for soprano and alto, one for tenor and bass, and one for the union of the four parts. The proficiency is indicated by the fact, that the pupils perform very creditably such compositions as ·Haydn's *Creation* and Handel's *Messiah*.

6. *Institute of Arts of Berlin..*

WINTER COURSE.

Monday. First Class, first division — drawing and sketching machines, eight A. M. to twelve o'clock. Discussion of machines, estimates of power, etc., two P. M. to five P. M. Second division — machine drawing, eight to ten. Modeling in clay, ten to twelve. Physics, two to five.

Second Class. Machine drawing, eight to ten. Modeling, ten to twelve. Elements of geometry, two to four. Repetition of the lecture, four to five.

Tuesday. First Class, first division — architectural plans and estimates, eight to twelve. Practical instruction in machinery, two to five. Second division — ornamental and architectural drawing, eight to twelve. Trigonometry, two to five.

Second Class. Ornamental and architectural drawing, eight to twelve. Physics, two to four. Repetition of the lecture, four to five.

Wednesday. First Class, first division — original designs, eight to twelve. Discussion of machinery. Second division — mineralogy, eight to nine. Machine drawing, nine to twelve. Trigonometry, two to five.

Second Class. Machine drawing, eight to twelve. Practical arithmetic, two to five.

Thursday. First Class, first division — drawing and sketching machines, eight to twelve. Architectural instruction, estimates, two to five. Second division — decorative and architectural drawing, eight to ten. Modeling in clay, ten to twelve. Trigonometry, two to five.

Second Class. Decorative and architectural drawing, eight to ten. Modeling in clay, ten to twelve. Physics, two to four. Repetition of the lecture, four to five.

Friday. First Class, first division — architectural plans, eight to twelve. Practical instruction in machinery, two to five. Second division — machine drawing, eight to twelve. Physics, two to five.

Second Class. Machine drawing, eight to twelve. Elementary mathematics, two to four. Repetition of the lessons, four to five.

Saturday. First Class, first division — perspective and stone-cutting, eight to twelve. Original designs, two to five. Second division — mineralogy, eight to nine. Decorative and architectural drawing, nine to twelve. Trigonometry, two to five.

Second Class. Decorative and architectural drawing, eight to twelve. Practical arithmetic, two to five.

The summer term, which follows this, embraces the practical instruction.

SUMMER TERM.

Monday. First Class, first division — in the workshops from seven A. M. to twelve, and from one until seven P. M. Second division — machine drawing, eight to twelve. Applied mathematics, two to five.

Second Class. Machine drawing, eight to ten. Modeling, ten to twelve. Chemistry, two to four. Repetition, four to five.

Tuesday. First Class, first division — analytical dynamics, eight to ten. Drawing of machines from original designs, nine to twelve. Machinery, two to five. Second division — decorative and architectural drawing, eight to twelve. Chemistry, two to five.

Second Class. Decorative and architectural drawing, eight to twelve. Elementary mathematics, two to four. Repetition, four to five.

Wednesday. First Class, first division — in the workshops from seven to twelve, and from one to seven. Second division — machine drawing, eight to ten. Modeling, ten to twelve. Applied mathematics, two to five.

Second Class. Machine drawing, eight to twelve. Practical arithmetic, two to four. Materials used in the arts, four to five.

Thursday. First Class, first division — in the workshops from seven to twelve, and from one to seven. Second division — machine drawing, eight to ten. Modeling, ten to twelve. Applied mathematics, two to five.

Second Class. Decorative and architectural drawing, eight to ten. Modeling, ten to twelve. Chemistry, two to four. Repetition of the lesson, four to five.

Friday. First Class, first division — analytical dynamics, eight to nine. Drawing of a machine for an original design, nine to twelve. Machinery, two to five. Second division — chemistry, eight to nine. Applied mathematics, nine to twelve. Chemistry, two to five.

Second Class. Machine drawing, eight to twelve. Elementary mathematics, two to four. Repetition of the lesson, four to five.

Saturday. First Class, first division — in the workshops, from seven to twelve, and from one to seven. Second division — decorative and architectural drawing, eight to twelve. Applied mathematics, two to five.

Second Class. Decorative and architectural drawing, eight to twelve. Practical arithmetic, two to four. Materials used in the arts, four to five.

The chemical division of the practical classes is engaged every day in the laboratory. On Tuesday and Wednesday, the library is open for reading from five to eight, P. M.

The collections for carrying out the various branches of instruction are upon the same liberal scale with the other parts of the institution. There is a library of works on architecture, mechanics, technology, the various arts, archaeology, etc., in German, French, and English. This library is open twice a week, from five to eight in the evening, to the pupils of the first class of the school, and to such mechanics as apply for the use of it.

There is a rich collection of drawings of new and useful machines, and of illustrations of the different courses, belonging to the institution. Among them is a splendid work, entitled Models for Manufacturers and Artisans, (Vorlegeblätter für Fabricanten und Handwerker) containing engravings by the best artists of Germany, and some even from France and England, applicable to the different arts and to architecture and engineering. Among the drawings are many from original designs by Shenckel, of Berlin. There is a second useful but more ordinary series of engravings, on similar subjects, also executed for the use of the school. These works are distributed to the provincial trade schools, and presented to such of the mechanics of Prussia as have especially distinguished themselves in their vocation. The collection of models of machinery belonging to the school probably ranks next in extent and value to that at the Conservatory of Arts of Paris. It contains models of such machines as are not readily comprehended by drawings. Most of them are working models, and many were made in the workshops of the school. They are constructed, as far as possible, to a uniform scale, and the parts of the models are of the same materials as in the actual machine. There is an extensive collection of casts, consisting of copies of statues, basso-relievos, utensils, bronzes, and vases of the museums of Naples, Rome, and Florence, and of the British Museum, and of the models of architectural monuments of Greece, Rome, Pompeii, etc., and copies of models, cameos, and similar objects; those specimens only have been selected which are not in the collection of the Academy of Fine Arts of

Berlin, to which the pupils of the Institute of Arts have access. There are good collections of physical and chemical apparatus, of minerals, of geological and technological specimens.

The instruction is afforded in part by the lectures of the professors, aided by text books specially intended for the school, and in part by the interrogations of the professors and of the assistants and repeaters. At the close of the first year there is an examination to determine which of the pupils shall be permitted to go forward, and at the close of the second year to determine which shall receive the certificate of the institute. Although the pupils who come from the provinces are admitted to the first class of the institute, upon their presenting a testimonial that they have gone through the course of the provincial schools satisfactorily, it frequently happens that they are obliged to retire to the second, especially from defective knowledge of chemistry.

The cost of this school to the government is about twelve thousand dollars annually, exclusive of the amount expended upon the practical courses and upon the collections — a very trifling sum, if the good which it is calculated to do throughout the country is considered.

Catalogue of Lectures Delivered in the Polytechnical School at Hanover.

PREPARATORY SCHOOL.

		Hours.
Low Mathematics,	Grelle,	
"	Guthe,	} 10
Theology and Botany,	Mühlenpfardt,	
Mineralogy,	Guthe,	
Sketching,	Schulz, Blank, Küsler,	} 15
Outline,	Bruns,	4

PRINCIPAL SCHOOL.

		Hours.
High Mathematics,	Grelle,	7
Geometry,	Slegemann, Büsing,	} 5
Practical Geometry,	Hunäus, Busing,	} 10
Mechanics, I course,	Ritter,	8
" II course,	"	7
Construction of machinery,	Grove,	
" I course,	"	5
" II course,	"	5
Theory of machinery,	Rühlmann,	
" I course,	"	5
" II course,	"	5
Architecture, I course.		
Constructions and Material,	Debo, Güer,	} 6
Ornamental,	Lüer,	4

		Hours.
Theory of Form and Perspective,	Köhler,	7
To sketch buildings,	Hase, Köhler,	11
Delivery,	Debo, Güer,	} 6
Ornamental,	Güer,	3
History of Architecture,	Hase,	4
Roads, Rail-Road Constructions,	v. Kaven,	12
Water-works,	Trenting,	13
Con. of Bridges,	Trenting, V. Kaven,	34
Geognosy,	Hunäus,	3
Theoretical Physics,	v. Quintus Talius,	5
Practical Physics,	"	5
Theoretical Chemistry,	Heeren,	5
Technical Chemistry,	"	5

PRACTICAL CHEMISTRY.

		Hours.
Experimenting in the Laboratory,	Kraut,	22
Analytic Chemistry,	Kraut,	3
Mechanical Technology,	Karmarsch, Hoyer,	} 5
Embossing works,	Engelhardt,	5
Moulding works,	Bruns,	5

Catalogue of the Lectures to be Delivered in the Frederick William University at Berlin, from Oct. 15, 1868, till March 19, 1869.

THEOLOGY.

By Prof. Dr. Hengstenberg: Hours.
The Introduction to the canonical books Old Testament, ... 5
The Prophecies of Isaiah, ... 5
The History of the Passion and Resurrection of Christ according to the four Gospels. 2

By Prof. Gic. Vatke:
The Introduction to the Old Testament, ... 5
The Origin of the Pentateuch, ... 1

By Prof. Benary:
Genesis, ... 5
The Book of the Judges, ... 1

By Gic. Kranichfeld:
Genesis, ... 5
The Book of Daniel, ... 2

Homiletic Exercises, Exercises in the Arabian and Hebrew language, ...

By Gic. Gerlach:
The Psalms, ... 5
Difficult Parts of the Old Testament explained in the Latin Language, 2

By Prof. Dr. Rödiger: Hours.
The Book of Job, ... 4
Solomon's Song, ... 1

By Prof. Dr. Dieterici:
The Lesser Prophets, ... 2

By Prof. Gic. Strauss:
Biblical Archæology, ... 2
Homiletics, ... 1
Homiletic Exercises, ... 1
Catechetical Exercises, ... 1

By Prof. Dr. Dorner:
The Gospel of John, ... 5
The Christian Symbolism, ... 5

By Prof. Dr. Frommann:
The Epistle to the Romans, ... 5
The Homiletics, ... 3

By Prof. Dr. Twesten:
The Epistles to the Thessalonians, Galatians, Philippians, Colossians, Ephesians, ... 5
The Principles of the Dogmatical Interpretations of the New Testament, ... 1
Christian Dogma, ... 6

By Prof. Gic. MESSNER: Hours.
  Parts of the Revelations, ... 1
  The Biblical Theology of the New
    Testament, ... 5
By Prof. Dr. PIPER:
  The 2d part of the Church History, ... 5
  The Archæological and Patristic Ex-
    ercises, ... 2
By Prof. Gic. WEINGARTEN:
  The 2d part of the Church History, .. 5
  The History of the Reformation, ... 2
By Prof. Dr. SEMISCH:
  The 3d part of the History of the
    Church, ... 6
  The Christian History of Dogma, ... 6
By Gic. PREUSS:
  The Apology of Christianity, ... 5
  A Disputation on the Augsburg Con-
    fession, ... 1
By Prof. Dr. STEINMETER:
  Practical Theology, ... 5
  The Catechetics, ... 1
  Homiletic Advices, ... 1
By Gic. KLEINERT:
  Theological Disputations, ... 1

JURISPRUDENCE.

By Prof. HYDEMANN:
  Encyclopædia or Methodologia of
    Jurisprudence, ... 3
  The Prussian Common Law, ... 5
  Disputations on Prussian and French
    laws, ... 2
  The Code Napoleon, ... 3
By Prof. BERNER:
  Law by Nature, ... 4
  Laws of Nations (International Law), 3
  German law of Punishment (penal
    justice), ... 4
  Penalty Process, ... 2
  Criminal Psychology, ... 1
By Prof. MICHELET:
  Law by Nature in connection with
    Universal History of Law, ... 4
By Prof. RUDORFF:
  Institutions and Antiquities of the
    Roman Law, ... 5
  History of the Roman State Law, ... 1
By Dr. SCHMIDT:
  Encyclopædia or Methodologia of
    Jurisprudence, ...
  On the Pandects and International
    History of the Roman law, also Ex-
    egetic Exercises., ... 6
By Dr. BARON:
  Institutions and Antiquities of the
    Roman Law, ... 4
  History of the Roman State law, ... 4
  Dogmatical and Exegetical Exercises
    on the Roman law, ... 1
  The Prussian Common Law, ... 5
By Dr. DEGENKOLL:
  Institutions and Antiquities of the
    Roman law, ... 5
  Practical exercises, ... 1
By Dr. ECK:
  Institutions of the Roman law, ... 4
  History of the Roman State law, ... 4
  Selected Civil law Cases, ... 1

By Dr. RYCK: Hours.
  Institutions of the Roman law, ... 4
  Law of inheritance, ... 2
By Prof. BRUNS:
  Practical law of pandects, ... 6
  Law of Inheritance, ... 3
  Selected Pandects, ... 1
By Prof. GNEIST:
  Law of Inheritance, ... 3
  History of the English Constitution, 1
  Common and Prussian Civil Law, ... 4
By Prof. HEFFTER:
  Canon Law, ... 4
  The Public Law of Prussia and other
    German States, ... 4
By Dr. HUBLER:
  Canon Law, ... 2
  Canonical Civil Law, ... ?
By Prof. HOMEYER:
  History of the German Empire and
    Law, ... 2
By Prof. KÜHNS:
  History of the German Empire and
    Law, ... 2
  German Law concerning Bills of Ex-
    change, ... 1
  Exercises of the German law, especi-
    ally of the Commercial Law, ... 1
  German Statute Law, ... 4
By Dr. LEWIS:
  History of the German Empire and
    Law, ... 4
  Definition of the Sachsenspiegel, ... 2
By Dr. GIERKE:
  History of the German Empire and
    Law, ... 2
By Dr. BEHREND:
  Definition of the Sachsenspiegel, ... 1
  German Statute Law, ... 5
  German Commercial Maritime and
    Exchange Law, ... 4
  On Exchange and Banking Business, 1
By Prof. BESELER:
  German Statute law including the
    Feudal, Commercial, Exchange
    and Maritime Law, ... 5
  German Law, ... 1
By Prof. V. HOLTZENDORFF:
  State Law, regarding especially the
    Documents of the Prussian Consti-
    tution, ... 4
  Politic and Common State Law, ... 2
  Common German and Prussian
    Penal Justice, ... 4
  Penalty Process, ... 2
  On Death Penalty, ... 1
By Prof. HINSCHIUS:
  Prussian Family Law, ... 1

MEDICAL SCIENCE.

By Prof. SCHULZ SCHUBZENSTEIN:
  Encyclopædia and Methodologia of
    the Medical Science, ... 2
  General Pathology and Therapeutics, 4
  Remedy Theory; Essays of the Effect
    of Medicine on Animals, ... 6
By Prof. HIRSCH:
  General History of Medical Science, 3
  General Pathology and Therapeutics, 5

62

By Prof. REICHERT: Hours.
Anatomy, ... 6
Anatomy of the Brain and Spinal
Marrow, ... 1
The Theoretical Histology,.......... 1
A Microscopical Anatomical Course, ?
Dissections, ... 12

By Prof. HARTMANN:
The Osteology and Syndesmology of
Man, ... 2
Anatomy of the Power of Senses,.... 1

By Prof. DU BOIS-REYMOND:
The 2d part of Physiology,.......... 5
Physiological Exercises in the Phy-
siological Laboratory, assisted by
Prof. Rosenthal,.................. ?

By Prof. ROSENTHAL:
The Experimental Part of Physio-
logy, ... 2
Theory of Electricity,.............. 1

By Dr. MUNK:
Selected Chapters of Physiology,.. 4
Physical and Physiological Base of
the Electrotherapy, with experiments, ... 1

By Dr. HERMANN:
About the Physiological Effects of
Gas, with experiments,.......... 1
Medical Chemistry, with experi-
ments,............................ 2
Physiological and Pathological
Chemical Tasks,.................. ?
The Theory of Poison, ... 2

By Dr. SIEBREICH:
Chemistry of Digestion,............ 1
Practical Medical Chemical Course,
with experiments,................ 3

By Prof. VIRCHOW:
General Pathology and Therapy, including General Pathological Anatomy, ... 4
A Demonstrative Course of Pathology, Anatomy and Microscopy
with advice to Pathological Sections,............................. 3
Practical Courses of the whole Medical Diagnosis, ...

By Dr. WESTPHAL:
Percussion and Auscultation, with
practical exercises,.............. ?
Laryngoscopic Course,............. ?

By Prof. LEWIN:
Syphilis,.......................... ?
The Clinical Medicine of Syphilitic
and Cutaneous Diseases,......... 3
Laryngoscopy, with practical exer-
cises,............................. 1
Auscultation, Percussion and Laryn-
goscopy, with demonstrations,.... ?

By Dr. WALDENBURG:
Laryngoscopy, with practical exer-
cises,............................. 1
Practical Course on Auscultation,
Percussion and Laryngoscopy,... 3

By Dr. EULENBURG:
Demonstrations of Diseases of the
Nerves, with practical exercises;
for three months,................ 4
Electrotherapy,...................

By Prof. GRIESINGER:
Clinical Medicine of the Diseases of
Nerves and Mental Debilities,.... 5

By Prof. MITSCHERLICH: Hours.
The Theory of Remedy,............ 6
On the Agitating Remedies,........ 2
General, and Special Surgery with
demonstrations, ...

By Dr. HELFT:
On Medical Climatology,........... 1
On the Use of Medical Springs for
Chronic Diseases,................ 4

By Dr. VALENTINER:
On the Medical Use of Mineral Water
for Chronic Diseases,............. 2

By Prof. YUNGKEN:
General and Special Surgery,...... 4
On the Ruptures of the Human Body, 2

By Dr. FISCHER:
General and Special Surgery,...... 4
On Ruptures in the Abdomen and
their Treatment,................. 2

By Prof. V. LANGENBECK:
Chirurgery, with surgical anatomi-
cal demonstrations,.............. 3
Surgical-Clinical-Medicine in the
Royal Surgical University Clini-
cum,.............................. 5

By Dr. RAVOTH:
On Chirurgery,...... .... ?

By Prof. GURLT:
Dissections,....................... 6
The Theory of Osteoceles and Dislo-
cations,.......................... 2

By Prof. V. GRAFE:
The Eye—its Diseases and Remedies,............................. 9

By Prof. BOHM:
Eyeglasses and their Medical Effects, 1

By Dr. ERHARD:
Diseases of the Auditory Nerve in
connection with demonstrations, 1

By Dr. LUCAE:
On the Eye and Ear, with demonstrations and experiments,...... 1

By Prof. ALBRECHT:
Diseases of the Teeth and Mouth,.. 2

By Prof. MARTIN:
Gynæcology and Midwifery,....... 5
Clinical and Policlinical Medicine in
connection with Midwifery and
Gynæcology,..................... 6

By Prof. EBERT:
Policlinical and Clinical Medicines
of Diseases of Children,.......... 3

MEDICAL JURISPRUDENCE.

By Prof. LIMAN:
Dissections,...................... ?

By Prof. SKRZECZKA:
Dissections, ... ?
Medical Jurisprudence,........... 6
Selected Chapters of the Medical
police,........................... 2

By Dr. SCHULTZ:
Medical Climatology,.............. 2
On the Climate of Italy,........... 1

PHILOSOPHICAL SCIENCES.

By Prof. TRENDELENBURG:
General History of Philosophy,.... 5
Psychology,....................... 4
Explanation of Aristotle's 2d Book
of Physics, in the Philosophical
Exercises,........................ 2

By Prof. ALTHAUS: Hours.
General History of Philosophy, up
to the 18th century,.............. 4
History of Philosophy from the be-
ginning of the 18th century,...... 2
Encyclopædia of the Philosophical
Sciences, including Logic,........ 4

By Prof. GRUPPE:
History of Greek Philosophy,...... 2

By Dr. MARKER:
Natural Philosophy of the Ancients,
according to Aristotle's Physics, 4

By Prof. MICHELET:
Logic and Encyclopædia of the
Philosophical Sciences,.......... 4
Philosophical Conservatory Disputa-
tion,........................... 1

By Prof. HARMS:
Logic and Metaphysics,.......... 4
Practical Philosophy, or Ethics,.... 4
Philosophical Exercises,.......... 1

By Dr. DUHRING:
Logic, combined with a course of
Philosophy, according to the prin-
ciples of Natural Dialectics,...... 4
Philosophical Privatissimis, ... 4

By Prof. WERDER:
Psychology and Anthropology,..... 3

By Prof. STEINTHAL:
Philosophy of Language and General Grammar,.................... 4

By Prof. MASSMANN:
Pedagogical Questions,............ 2

MATHEMATICAL SCIENCES.

By Prof. KUMMER:
Theory of Numbers,.............. 4

By Dr. KRONECKER:
Theory of Algebraic Algebra,...... 2

By Prof. WEIERSTRASS:
Theory of the Elliptical Functions, 6

By Prof. FUCHS:
Theory of the Differential and Integral Calculus,................... 4

By Dr. HOPPE:
Integral Calculus,............... 4
Analytic Geometry,.............. 4

By Prof. OHM:
Analytic Mechanics,.............. 3

By Prof. FORSTER:
Selected chapters, Astronomical Me-
chanics,....................... 4
The History of Astronomy,........ 2

By Dr. AUWERS:
The Double Stars,............... 2

THE PHYSICAL SCIENCES.

By Prof. POGGENDORF:
General History of Physics; from
Galileo to the present time,...... 2

By Prof. MAGNUS:
Physics with Essays,............. 5
Practical Physical Exercises,....... ?
Physical Colloquia,............... ?

By Prof. DOVE:
Experimental Physics,.. 2
Meteorology,.................... 2

By Prof. ERMAN: Hours.
Physics of the Earth; or the Theory
of the Geographical and Cosmo-
graphical Phenomenon,.......... 3
Theoretical and Practical Advices
regarding Scientific and Physical
Observations,................... ?

By Prof. GUINCKE:
Theory of Electricity,............ 4
Optics,......................... 2

By Dr. PAALZOW:
Mechanical Theory of Warmness,... 1

By Dr. OPPENHEIM:
The History of Chemistry of our Age, 2
Organic Chemistry,.............. 3

By Dr. SONNENSCHEIN:
The History of Chemistry,......... 1
Judicial Chemistry, with Essays,.... 2
Practical Chemical Tasks,......... 6
Chemical Colloquia,............. ?

By Dr. REMELE:
History of Analytic Chemistry,..... 1
The Quantitative Parts of Analytic
Chemistry, with experiments,.... 3
Chemical Mineralogy,............ 3

By Prof. HOFMANN:
Experimental Chemistry,.......... 3
Introduction to Analytic Chemistry, 1
Chemical Experimental Exercises,.. 6

By Dr. WICHELHAUS:
Organic Chemistry,.............. 4
Scientific Chemical Researches,.... 6

By Prof. SCHNEIDER:
Organic Chemistry, especially for
Medicine and Pharmacy,........ 5
Organic Bases, ... 1
Inorganic Pharmacy,............ 3
Practical Chemical Exercises,....... 6
Summary of Zoology,.............. 3
Natural History of Tape-worms of
Man,......................... 5
A Zoological Course directed by him

By Prof. BAEYER:
The 2d part of Organic Chemistry,
with experiments,.............. 4
Practical Exercises on Organic Chemistry,........................ 6

By Prof. RAMMELSBERG:
The 1st part of Special Inorganic
Chemistry,..................... 4
The Chemical Principles of Metal-
lurgy,......................... 3

By Prof. ROSE:
Mineralogy, ... 6
Crystallography,................ 1

By Prof. BEYRICH:
Petrifications,.................. 4
Geognosy with regard to Mountains
formed in Horizontal Layers,..... 2

By Prof. ROTH:
Geology,....................... 2
Volcanoes,..................... 1

By Dr. LASPEYRES:
General Petrography, ... 4

By Prof. BRAUN:
General Botany, regarding especially
Medical and Economical Plants,.. 5
Exercises to determine Cryptogami-
cal Plants,.................... ?
Botanical Conservatory, ... ?

By Prof. KARSTEN: Hours.
Medical Botany showing Medical
  Plants and Drugs,................. 6
Pharmacognosy, ... 4
Anatomical Physical Exercises,..... ?

By Dr. KNY:
Fructification of Plants, ... 2
Anatomical and Physical Exercises, 5

By Prof. PETERS:
General and Special Zoology,....... 6
Zoological Zootomic Exercises,..... 2

By Dr. GERSTACKER:
General and Special Entomology
with Microscopical Demonstra-
tions, ... 3

By Prof. DU BOIS REYMOND:
Physical Anthropology, ... 1

SCIENCES OF STATE FINANCE AND
INDUSTRY.

By Prof. HANSSEN:
People's Political Economy,........ 4
Science of Finances, ... 4
Financial Exercises,................ 1

By Prof. FRIEDLAENDER:
National Economy,................. 4

By Dr. DÜHRING:
National Economy acording to Prin-
ciples of Critical Foundation, ... 4
Parties in the State and Society,.... 1
Political Eonomy, ...
Prussian Finances, Police and Ad-
ministration,....................

By Prof. HELWING:
Police Science or Theory of intrin- ⎫
sic Administration, also Theory ⎪
of State Economy, ⎬ 4
Agricultural, Industrious and Com- ⎪
mercial Police. ⎭
Examinations and Disputations on
the Science of Politics and Finances, ... ?

By Dr. SCHULZ:
Police, ... 2

By Prof. THAER:
Principles of Agricultural Credit and
Insurance,...................... 1
Agricultural Production of Animals, 4
Colloquia on Selected Parts of the
Practical Management of Agricul-
ture,. 1

By Prof. KOCH:
Agricultural Botany, with demonstrations on living plants,......... 2

By Dr. GERSTACKER:
Insects Pernicious and Useful to
Agriculture, ... 2

HISTORY AND GEOGRAPHY.

By Prof. V. RAUMER:
History of Constitutions and Politics, 1

By Prof. KOPKE:
History of the Middle Ages, ... 4
Historical Exercises, ... 1

By Dr. ERDMANNSDORFFER:
History from the end of the Middle
Ages with regard to Literature
and Civilization, ... 4
History of the English Revolution, 2

By Prof. V. RANKE: Hours.
History of the Present Age, since
the Declaration of Independence
of the United States of America, 4
Historical Exercises, ... ?

By Prof. DROYSEN:
History since 1815, ... 5
Greek History, ... 4
Exercises of the Historical Society, ?

By Dr. HASSEL:
History of Prussia from 1784–1815, 1

By Prof. TAFFE:
Historical Exercises,................ 1

By Prof. KIEPERT:
History of the Earth and Geographical Discoveries, ... 3

By Dr. BASTIAN:
History of Colonies from the 15th
Century till the present time, ... 1
Ethnology and Anthropology, ... 4

By Prof. MÜLLER:
Geography and Knowledge of Dif-
ferent States of the New World, 4
The History of the New World, ... 1

THEORY AND HISTORY OF ART.

By Prof. HOTHO:
Æsthetics, with a Summary on History of Art, ... 2

By Prof. WERDER:
On Dramatic Art, ... 1

By Dr. MAERCKER:
Rhetoric, ... 1
Rhetorical Exercises, ... 1

By Prof. CURTIS:
History of Plastic Arts of the Greeks,
and Romans. '..................... 5
Exercises of Classical Archæology
and Monuments, ... ?

By Prof. FRIEDERICHS:
History of Greek-Roman Art,........
Archæological Exercises,........... 1

By Prof. LEPSIUS:
Egyptian Monuments,.............. 1

By Prof. BELLERMANN:
History of Music of the middle ages,
from beginning of Christianity till
Franco of Cologne, 13th century,.. 2
Counterpoint Exercises,............ 2

PHILOLOGICAL SCIENCES AND EX-
PLANATION OF AUTHORS.

By Prof. STEINTHAL:
The style of the Indo-Germanic Lan-
guage, with regard to the Greek,
Latin and German Language,..... 4
History of the Science of the Lan-
guages of the Greeks and Romans, 1

By Prof. MASSMANN:
Science of Handwriting............ ?
Explains the Germania of Tacitus,. 4
Monuments regarding the Gothic
Languages, combined with the
History of the Gothic Language, 4

By Prof. KIRCHHOFF:
History of Greek Literature till time
of Alexander the Great,.......... 4
Explains Medea of Euripides,...... 4

By Prof. HAUPT:
Explains the Birds of Aristophanes, 4
Explains the Eunuchus of Terentius, 4

By Prof. MULLACH : Hours.
Explains Thucydides in the Latin
Language,............................ 1
Explains Cicero De Oratione,....... 4

By Prof. HUBNER ;
The Funeral Oration of Pericles over
Thucydides,...................... 1
History of Roman Literature,....... 4
On Roman Private Antiquities, with
the Help of Monuments of Art,... 3

By Prof. BEKKER :
Oration of Isocrates,................ 2

By Dr. BONITZ :
On the Life and Literary Works of
Plato, with the explanation of
the Dialogue, Theaetel,........... 2

By Prof. GEFFERT :
Roman Antiquities,................ 4
The Casina of Plautus,............. 2

By Prof. TAFFE :
Latin Paleography,................. 3

By Dr. MAERKER :
Lucrez's books, Treating the Things
of Nature,....................... 1

By Prof. MEMMSEN :
Selected Parts of Gaius's Institutions,........................... 1

By Prof. MULLENHOFF :
The Nibelunge Noth, ... 4
The Songs of the Old Edda,........ 4
The German Exercises to be con-
tinued,.......................... 1

By Prof. TOBLER :
French Grammar,.... 4
On the Novelas Ejemplares of Cer-
vantes,.......................... 2
Exercises of his Romanian Society, 1

By Lec. FABBRUCCI :
History of Italian Literature in the
Italian Language,................ 3
Italian Language,... 2
Offers an Italian and French course,
Privatissimis ....

By Lec. SOLLY :
History of English Literature from
15th century, in the English Lan-
guage,........................... 1
Offers a Privatissimis in the English
Language........................

By Prof. WEBER :
Sanskrit Grammar,................. 3
Explains Bhavabhûtis Mâlatimâd-
hava,...... 2
Hymns of Rigveda or Atharvaveda, 3
Zend, or Pali Grammar,............ 2
Offers Privatissimis in Sanskrit,
Pâli or Zend................. .....

By Dr. TOHAENTGEN ; Hours.
The Grammatical Sûtra of Pânini,.. 2

By Dr. HAARBRUCKER ;
The Syrian Language,.............. 2
The Arabian Language,............. 3

By Prof. RODIGER :
Solomon's Song,................... 1
The Book of Job,.................. 4
The Koran and other Arabian tenets,
also the Arabian Syntax,......... 3
Offers Privatissimis for the Hebrew,
Arabian or Ethiopian language...

By Prof. DIETERICI :
Grammar of the Arabian language, 3
Explains some Arabian Authors,.... 1

By Lic. Dr. KRANICHFELD :
Grammar of the Arabian language,
with practical exercises,........ 2

By Dr. WETZSTEIN :
On the Idiom of the Zeltaraber,.... 1
On the Lyric Poetry of the Arabians, 2

By Prof. BENARY :
The Hebrew language and the other
similar Dialects, Privatissimis....

By Prof. LEPSIUS :
Egyptian Grammar,................ 3

By Dr. PIETRASZEWSKI :
The Persian Grammar, and Zend
Language, also the Polish and
Russian Language,................ 2
The Turkish Grammar with Trans-
lation of Kirk Wezir,............. 2
Offers Privatissimis in the Persian
and Turkish Language............

By Prof. SCHOTT :
On the Literature of People of Fin-
land Descent,.................... 2
The Finland (Suomi) Language,.... 2
The Chinese Language,............. 2

By Lec. MICHAELIS :
German Stenography, with Practical
Exercises,....................... 2
Practical Stenographical Exercises, 1
Offers Privatissimis in the German,
English and French Stenography..
On the Principles of the German
Orthography,.................... 1

GYMNASTICS.

Mr. NEUMANN teaches Fencing.
Mr. FREISING " Dancing.
Mr. HILDEBRANDT " Riding horseback.

PUBLIC INSTITUTIONS.

To the Royal Library, and University Library, every student is admitted. The
Observatory, the Botanic Garden, Anatomical Zoological and Zoological
Museum, the Herbarium, the Mineral
Department, the Collection of Surgical
Instruments and Bandages, the Physical Apparatus, the Pharmacological
Collection, the Collection of Charts of
the Royal Chartographic Institution,
the Christian Archæological Collection
of the University, the Museum of Arts,
the Collection of Plaster Casts, the
Archæological Collection of the University, can be used during the course.

The Exegetical Exercises of the Theological Seminary, regarding the New Testament, will be directed by Prof. Dr· TWESTON; those of the Old Testament by Prof. Dr. HENGSTENBERG; those of the History of the Church and Dogmas by Prof. Dr. SEMISH. The following Institutions are for the study of Medicine and Surgery.

The Anatomical Theatre and Physiological Laboratory, the Medical, Surgical Polclinical Institution, the Clinicum for Surgery and Medical Science for Eyes, the Clinicum of the University, for Midwifery, the Policlinic for Midwifery, the Clinical Department of the Charitè Hospital, as the Operation Cliniucm for Surgery, the Clinicum for Medical Science for Eyes, and ¦Perfection of Oculists, the Clinicum for Syphilitic Patients, Psychiatric Clinicum and the Clinicum for the Disease of the Nerves, the Clinicum for Midwifery and Treatment of Women lying-in, and New-born Children, the Pathological Institution in the Charitè, and the Department for Practical Exercises of Judicial Medicine, in the Anatomical building.

In the Philosophical Seminary under the direction of Prof. HAUPT, the Dialogue of Tacitus will be explained every Wednesday.

The Orations of Lysias will be explained under the direction of Prof. KIRCHHOFF, every Saturday.

The Disputation Exercises will be directed also by Prof. KIRCHHOFF.

The Exercises of the Mathematical Seminary will be directed by Prof. KUMMER and Prof. WEIERSTRASS.